The Florida Keys
The Natural Wonders of an Island Paradise

Text by Jeff Ripple
Photographs by Bill Keogh and Jeff Ripple

Voyageur Press

Edited by Mary Katharine Parks
Designed by Kathryn Mallien
Printed in Hong Kong
95 96 97 98 99 5 4 3 2 1

Library of Congress Cataloging-in-Publication Data:
Ripple, Jeff, 1963–
     The Florida Keys : the natural wonders of an island paradise / text by Jeff Ripple ; photographs by Jeff Ripple and Bill Keogh ; forewords by Bob Graham and Irene Hooper.
          p. cm.
     Includes bibliographical references and index.
     ISBN 0-89658-262-0
     1. Florida Keys (Fla.)—Description and travel. 2. Florida Keys (Fla.)—Guidebooks. 3. Natural history—Florida—Florida Keys.
     I. Keogh, Bill. II. Title.
     F317.M7R57 1994
     917.59'—dc20   94-29896
          CIP

Distributed in Canada by Raincoast Books, 8680 Cambie Street, Vancouver, B.C. V6P 6M9

Published by Voyageur Press, Inc.
P.O. Box 338, 123 North Second Street, Stillwater, MN 55082 U.S.A.
612-430-2210, fax 612-430-2211

Please write or call, or stop by, for our free catalog of natural history publications. Our toll-free number to place an order or to obtain a free catalog is 800-888-WOLF (800-888-9653).

Educators, fundraisers, premium and gift buyers, publicists, and marketing managers: Looking for creative products and new sales ideas? Voyageur Press books are available at special discounts when purchased in quantities, and special editions can be created to your specifications. For details contact our marketing department.

Front and back cover photos © Bill Keogh. PAGE 1: *A bar jack cruising the clear blue waters of the Gulf Stream. (Photo © Bill Keogh)* PAGES 2–3: *Sunset colors the sky and clouds over Big Pine Key, National Key Deer Refuge. (Photo © Jeff Ripple)* PAGE 6: *Red mangroves silhouetted against the sunset, National Key Deer Refuge. (Photo © Jeff Ripple)*

For Renée

A reddish egret (white phase) feeding in a salt pond.
(Photo © Bill Keogh)

Acknowledgments

I am indebted to the following people and organizations for reviewing chapters, sharing their knowledge, providing guidance, and helping me to gain a clearer view of life in the Keys: Jeanne Parks and Pat Wells (Florida Park Service); Bill and Sande Haynes; Harold Hudson, Kady Crist, Lauri MacLaughlin, and Paige Gill (National Oceanic and Atmosphere Administration); John Swanson and Bill Gibbs (Keys Marine Laboratory); Mike Ross; Curtis Kruer; Ann Williams; Jorge Newbery ("Solar George," our fearless pilot); Paul Moler (Florida Game and Fresh Water Fish Commission); National Audubon Society (Florida Keys Office); SeaCamp/Newfound Harbor Marine Institute; The Nature Conservancy; Florida Keys Land and Sea Trust; REEF RELIEF; and the National Key Deer Refuge. Bill Keogh has been an exceptional guide and friend; his photographic contributions to the book are much appreciated. Finally, my deepest thanks to my lovely wife Renée, for her companionship in the field, her editorial comments on drafts of the chapters, her patience and good humor, and above all else, for believing in me.

Contents

Land hermit crabs warring over shells in a hardwood hammock
on Big Pine Key, National Key Deer Refuge.
(Photo © Bill Keogh)

Foreword by Senator Bob Graham

Key deer on one of the outer islands of the Newfound Harbor Keys.
(Photo © Bill Keogh)

Ever since I was a child growing up in South Florida, I have loved the Florida Keys. The clear blue waters and breathtaking scenery have drawn me back when I have been away too long. To me, the Keys are beautiful, natural, and, no matter how familiar, always capable of surprise.

After learning to scuba dive a couple of years ago, I realized that there is much more to the Keys than I knew. The Keys house countless land and sea wonders that go largely unnoticed at first glance, but contribute to their intrigue when discovered.

Visitors might be deceived by the topography of the Keys. By observing the tops of mangrove trees and other indigenous plants, one might conclude that the Keys are flat. Beneath the water's surface, however, there are enormous variations in landscape. Canyons, jutting mounds, and running hedges of coral reef are surrounded and intertwined by schools of fish often clustered so close together that they block out the light from above.

Despite their linear appearance, the Keys are actually a scattering of islands covering almost three thousand square nautical miles of breathtaking sea. Only the convenience of railroad engineers laying out the path of Henry Flagler's railbridge to Key West created the artificially straight character.

The Keys, so clear and clean, might also appear to have been discovered just years ago. Actually, the Keys represent some of the oldest inhabited areas in North America. Native American tribes, on their way to America from the Caribbean islands, encountered this wondrous maze of islands before reaching the mainland.

The flag of virtually every European nation has flown over the Keys at some point during the centuries of conquest and discovery. Many of these nations' ships still lie at the bottom of the coral reefs, providing an underwater museum of our nation's history. Relics of America's natural and man-made history can be found throughout the Keys in places such as Lignum Vitae, Indian Key, and Fort Jefferson in the Dry Tortugas.

My love for the Keys has made me a strong advocate for their preservation. That is why I introduced legislation passed by Congress in 1990 that established the Florida Keys National Marine Sanctuary. Vessel grounding, water pollution, and human contact have begun to leave their mark on the spectacular coral reefs. Fish catches have dropped and algae has begun to cloud the clear blue waters.

The Keys are a scattering of islands covering almost three thousand square nautical miles of breathtaking sea

By designating the area a sanctuary, Congress protected marine animals and plants, and their habitats. Now, oil and gas drilling is forbidden, and large tankers and freighters are prohibited from getting too close to the fragile reefs. But at the same time, the law permits controlled commercial and sport fishing, diving, boating, and any other activities not injurious to the environment when performed properly.

The beneficiaries of this law, of course, are the people as well as the area itself. The people of the Keys are as interesting and eclectic as the ecology. These traits have become the basis for some of literature's most intriguing characters, such as Harry Morgan in Ernest Hemingway's *To Have and Have Not*.

I've had first-hand experience with the characteristic pride of the people of the Keys. While preparing to deliver the commencement speech at the Keys Community College graduation ceremony in 1982, I was told that the Keys had seceded from the Union and established the independent Conch Republic. Keys residents were protesting the establishment of a refugee checkpoint in the upper Keys by the U.S. Immigration Service. The proud people of the Keys figured that if they were going to be treated as a foreign country, they might as well be one. And while the Conch Republic was never officially formed, the spirit of independence remains.

The citizens of the Keys treasure the area in which they live, and so should we. If not protected, the Keys might fall to the deterioration that has gripped so many other natural landmarks in America. Appreciation and understanding of the Keys, as well as support for efforts at preservation, will give future generations the same opportunity to experience the Keys as do we.

—Senator Bob Graham

Foreword by Irene Hooper

Snowberry blossoms, Big Pine Key, National Key Deer Refuge.
(Photo © Jeff Ripple)

People who love the outdoors often find themselves wishing that they could preserve the "wholeness" of special outdoor experiences. This wholeness encompasses all the feelings, beliefs, and emotions that nature brings forth, living in our memories as special times and places. That Jeff Ripple and Bill Keogh have experienced such moments in the Florida Keys is evident in this book. Vivid descriptions and photographs of the corals, mangroves, wetlands, fishes, and fiddler crabs leave images in our imagination that remain long after our first experience with the book. Jeff's words offer gifts to our minds just as one would place a cherished family heirloom in the palm of another person's hand. It is evident in every paragraph and photograph that Jeff and Bill know and love the Keys.

A Cuban tree frog on a palmetto blade. This non-native (exotic) frog is only one of many species of plants and animals that have been accidentally or purposely introduced to the Florida Keys. Exotics thrive often to the detriment of native species. (Photo © Bill Keogh)

The Florida Keys—The Natural Wonders of an Island Paradise addresses the origins, natural history, and ecological importance of the Keys in a manner that entertains and educates. Residents and visitors alike are invited to share the challenges that must be faced to preserve the Keys for future generations of humans and animals. Jeff's text leads us to appreciate the scientific importance and interdependence of all the elements that make up the ecology of the Keys, including their place within Florida's diverse environment. The text is joined by photographs from Bill and Jeff to capture timeless moments in the Keys' natural history. The photographs bring to us in startling color many images that we may have never seen, regardless of our own time spent in the Keys. Both men spent weeks in the field to capture the essence of the Keys' landscape and its inhabitants.

The Keys are worth preserving not only for human use, but for their own sake and for reasons that humankind may not totally understand for many more decades. As Jeff states, "The ecology, economy, and quality of life in the Keys are intertwined and must be managed accordingly." This book carries a message of personal action and change. The future is not something we inherit, but something we create by banding together people who care. Many organized public and private groups are interested in preservation and sustainable development in the Keys. There is value in the diversity of their viewpoints and their dedication to solving problems. There is also value in the ideas of people who do not belong to formal groups, but who love the Keys and care about its water and land.

In the long run, it will be the thousands of individuals making small decisions regarding how to live their daily lives who will make workable the policies, scientific research, and education now underway in the Keys. The next generation will be left with many problems to solve that we could not. *The Florida Keys—The Natural Wonders of an Island Paradise* is a book that will stand as an example to our heirs that we cared enough to come together and create a future for the Keys.

—**Irene Hooper, Executive Director, SeaCamp/**
Newfound Harbor Marine Institute,
Big Pine Key, Florida

Preface

Sunset over Snipe Keys,
Great White Heron National Wildlife Refuge.
(Photo © Jeff Ripple)

The Florida Keys. Some call this 150-mile chain of islands at Florida's southern tip one of the most diverse and important ecological features of North America. Others simply call it "Paradise." The Keys attract an estimated four million visitors each year, many of whom come to dive and fish on the United States' only living coral reef tract. Most visitors, however, are unaware that there is much more to the nature of the Keys than the coral reefs. Wide expanses of seagrass beds, mysterious mangrove forests, lush tropical hardwood hammocks, rocky pinelands, and a variety of freshwater and saltwater wetlands are as much a part of the Keys as the reefs. The subtropical climate and proximity to the Gulf Stream have allowed a unique blend of West

Silversides schooling in a channel between a turtle grass bed and a mangrove island. (Photo © Bill Keogh)

economy, and the beauty and abundance of the islands' natural resources are the main attractions. In the frenzied rush to attract more people, protection for the environment has been considered secondary. The result? A unique ecological treasure is imperiled, and the very foundation of the Keys' economic health is eroding in the process.

In this book, I have tried to provide an entertaining yet thorough introduction to the ecology of the Keys, their plants and wildlife, and both the natural and human-caused challenges that face these islands. In doing so, I'm hoping that more people will understand how the natural environment of the Keys should function and why it is important to ensure that they are protected. I think that once a broad base of the population realizes what is happening in the Keys and why it is happening, there will be greater incentive for tackling the issues at hand. Then, perhaps, we will inch a little bit closer to finding solutions that will allow people to coexist with all things living and wild in the island paradise of the Florida Keys.

Indian and temperate plants and wildlife to become established on these coral islands. Many species are threatened or endangered, making the Keys an important repository of rare life forms.

As with nearly every ecological treasure in North America, the Florida Keys are faced with a formidable array of environmental threats. Development, pollution, and other human activities are taking their toll on fragile ecosystems, even those "protected" within the nearly twenty national and state parks, refuges, and sanctuaries established to preserve the Keys' natural heritage. Tourism is the driving force of the Keys'

Origins

A mangrove island and channel, Lower Florida Keys.
(Photo © Jeff Ripple)

From the vantage of a small chartered plane, I watched the backcountry waters surrounding the Content Keys unfold before me like a scarf of fine silk, a delicate, diaphanous wash of varied greens, indigo, and sand. Clear, calm shallows mirrored a pale thread of cumulus couched just above the horizon, and I could trace the sinuous line of a channel as it wound its way among mangrove islands and beds of turtle grass.

Geology has never been my strong suit, but from an altitude of one thousand feet, I was able to decipher at least the lay of the Keys. They sweep south in a graceful arc from Miami's Biscayne Bay past the tip of Florida, bounded on the north by Florida Bay and on the south by the Florida

Moon jellyfish congregating near a reef, Looe Key National Marine Sanctuary. (Photo © Bill Keogh)

Mangrove islands, channels, and sandbars in the Marvin Keys, Great White Heron National Wildlife Refuge. (Photo © Jeff Ripple)

GULF OF MEXICO

GREAT WHITE HERON
NATIONAL WILDLIFE
REFUGE

Dry Tortugas

DRY TORTUGAS
NATIONAL PARK

KEY WEST NATIONAL
WILDLIFE REFUGE

Key
West

STRAITS O

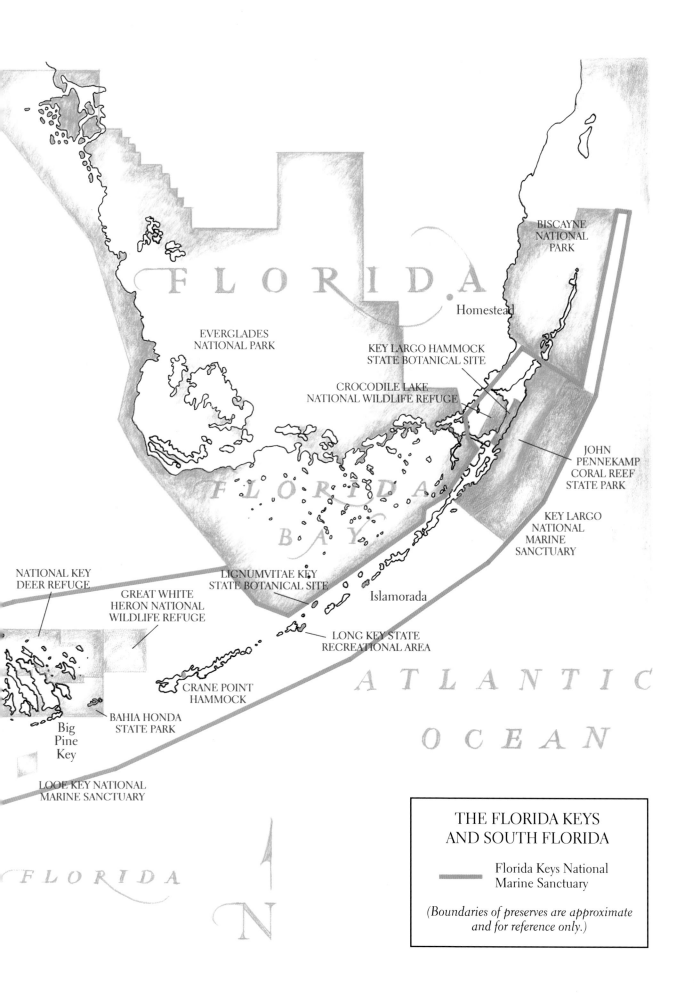

BISCAYNE
NATIONAL
PARK

F L O R I D A

Homestead

EVERGLADES
NATIONAL PARK

KEY LARGO HAMMOCK
STATE BOTANICAL SITE

CROCODILE LAKE
NATIONAL WILDLIFE REFUGE

JOHN
PENNEKAMP
CORAL REEF
STATE PARK

F L O R I D A

KEY LARGO
NATIONAL
MARINE
SANCTUARY

B A Y

NATIONAL KEY
DEER REFUGE

LIGNUMVITAE KEY
STATE BOTANICAL SITE

GREAT WHITE
HERON NATIONAL
WILDLIFE REFUGE

Islamorada

LONG KEY STATE
RECREATIONAL AREA

A T L A N T I C

CRANE POINT
HAMMOCK

BAHIA HONDA
STATE PARK

Big
Pine
Key

O C E A N

LOOE KEY NATIONAL
MARINE SANCTUARY

F L O R I D A

N

THE FLORIDA KEYS
AND SOUTH FLORIDA

Florida Keys National
Marine Sanctuary

*(Boundaries of preserves are approximate
and for reference only.)*

Straits, before gradually bending west into the Gulf of Mexico. The Upper Keys, which extend nearly 110 miles from Soldier Key to Big Pine Key, are oriented in a line along this arc from the north to the southwest. The Lower Keys, extending some forty miles from Big Pine to Key West, are oriented at almost right angles to the arc and are separated from each other by narrow channels that run in a northwest-southeast direction. In the Lower Keys, the islands are smaller and more numerous than those in the Upper Keys, giving rise to collective names for the hundreds of mangrove clumps in this area, including the Content Keys, the Saddlebunch Keys, the Snipe Keys, the Mud Keys, and the Sand Keys.

Our flight path took us over Big Pine Key along the dividing edge between the Upper and Lower Keys. I looked east from the cockpit toward the Seven-Mile Bridge and Marathon; to the west was Sugarloaf Key and beyond that, on the horizon, was Key West. Only minutes before, we had flown over Looe Key, the remarkable spur-and-groove coral reef just off the coast of Big Pine. Looe Key is only one of more than one hundred reefs that stretch along the seaward side of the Keys from Soldier Key to Key West. These reefs include Long Reef, Ajax, Triumph, Tennessee, Alligator, the Sambos, Carysfort, Molasses, French, Crocker's, Hen and Chickens, Turtle Rocks, Key Largo Dry Rocks, Sombrero, and American Shoals. They are legendary diving spots and are among the most visited reefs in the world.

Coral reefs have figured prominently in the development of the Keys, and as tranquil as the setting below me appeared, I knew it was a landscape in flux. Rachel Carson, in *The Edge of the Sea*, aptly describes the Keys as ". . . a coast not formed of lifeless rock or sand, but created by the activities of living things, which, though having bodies formed of protoplasm even as our own, are able to turn the substance of the sea into rock." The Keys are unusual because their development has been and remains biogenic or dependent on animal life. Prehistoric coral built the limestone foundation that is the ancient reef on which the Upper Keys now rest, while the limestone remains of

The Keys sweep south in a graceful arc from Miami's Biscayne Bay past the tip of Florida

calcareous algae are a significant component of the oolitic rock beneath the Lower Keys. Living corals today continue building the offshore reefs that may become the islands of tomorrow. Mangroves and calcareous algae continue to contribute to the outward expansion of the Keys.

Ancient Beginnings

The foundation of the Florida Keys as we know them today was laid during the latter part of the Pleistocene Epoch, a see-sawing of climatic and geologic forces marked by several periods of glaciation, or "Ice Ages," with intervening warming trends. During glaciation, the earth cooled, the polar caps expanded, and immense fields of ice ground their way south to cover much of North America and Europe. Sea level fell worldwide. During interglacial (warm) periods, the glaciers retreated, the polar caps receded, and sea level rose.

The ancient reefs that now underlie the Florida Keys are believed to have developed between 150,000 and 200,000 years ago during the last warm period of the Pleistocene—the Sangamon Interglacial. Sea level was approximately twenty-five feet higher than it is today, and warm ocean water bathed all of southern Florida. Living corals thrived on a platform reef that covered a shallow, submerged plateau at the edge of the continental shelf. This giant reef tract, reaching from what is present-day Miami to the Dry Tortugas, is now the Key Largo limestone that forms the surface bedrock of the Upper Keys from Soldier Key to Big Pine Key.

An extensive lagoon spread behind the Sangamon reef, covering what is now the freshwater Everglades. Bryozoans (mosslike creatures) thrived in these waters as encrustations on underwater plants. Ooids (egg-shaped calcareous particles of nonbiogenic origin) formed in areas of actively moving water, conditions that once prevailed along the Atlantic Coastal Ridge and in the Lower Keys. Currents kept the ooids suspended in the water column before they eventually grew heavy enough to settle to the bottom. These ooids and the skeletal remains of the bryozoans eventually

ABOVE: *Cap rock and Bahama morning glory, Big Pine Key, National Key Deer Refuge. (Photo © Jeff Ripple)* LEFT: *Gumbo limbo roots grip Key Largo limestone at the edge of a solution hole, Lignumvitae Key State Botanical Site. (Photo © Jeff Ripple)* OVERLEAF: *The calm waters of the backcountry wilderness mirror the buildup of a thunderhead over a mangrove island on a typical summer morning, National Key Deer Refuge. (Photo © Jeff Ripple)*

ABOVE: *A tropical hardwood hammock, National Key Deer Refuge. (Photo © Jeff Ripple)* RIGHT: *Seagrass and algae in a tidal pool, Great White Heron National Wildlife Refuge. (Photo © Jeff Ripple)*

consolidated to form the underlying layers of bedrock of our present-day Everglades and Florida Bay.

Some of the oolitic sediment drifted south to cover the coral at the lower, deeper end of the great reef tract. This sediment is now Miami limestone, the surface bedrock of the Lower Keys from Big Pine Key to Key West. The numerous natural channels separating the islands of the Lower Keys are the result of tidal water snaking through ancient oolitic sands on a course between the Florida Straits and the Gulf of Mexico. Key Largo limestone is covered by the layer of Miami limestone from Big Pine Key to Key West. Between Key West and the Dry Tortugas, it is covered by recent deposits of carbonate sands.

Sea level began to fall with the onset of the Wisconsin Glacier Period some 100,000 years ago, and southern Florida's coral reefs and surrounding marine sediments became dry ground. A short warming trend followed, but the cold returned and deepened. By the peak of glaciation 15,000 years ago, sea level had dropped 300 to 350 feet below what it is today. At that time, southern Florida and the Keys were a subtle, rolling topography cloaked with subtropical plant communities, pocked by solution holes (depressions or deep holes resulting from the dissolving of limestone by water mixing with acids from decaying vegetation). Coral and oolitic limestone exposed to rainwater and acids from decaying vegetation dissolved and then reprecipitated to create harder, denser "cap rock." This cap rock can be seen as smooth outcrops of limestone overlying the more textured Key Largo and Miami limestones throughout the Keys.

The Holocene Epoch marked a gradual warming trend that began with the retreat of the Wisconsin glaciers and continues today. The resulting rise in sea level brought about a resurgence of coral growth that commenced about ten thousand years ago along the coast of southeastern Florida. Approximately 5,500 years ago, Florida Bay was born, and it slowly spread over the land to commingle with the Gulf of Mexico and Atlantic Ocean, until only a scattered collection of more than two hundred mud banks and mangrove-fringed islands remained as testimony to the former expanse of dry ground. These last high spots are the Florida Keys. Hawk Channel, a deep channel running

parallel to the mainline keys (those connected by U.S. 1) between the inshore patch reefs and offshore bank reefs, also formed during this time.

The Nature of the Tides

The Keys lie low, barely breaking the ocean surface. Most of the islands rise only two to four feet above the level of high tide. On somber, stormy days, they sulk on the horizon, dark and sullen against gray, frothing seas. On bright, still, summer mornings, water and sky meld, and the backcountry islands sail on Florida Bay like Spanish frigates, with puffy cumulus clouds billowing up and outward like mainsails.

I have found that my impressions of the islands vary with the tide as much as with weather conditions. At low tide, many of the mudflats are covered with wading birds stalking the shallows or newly exposed mud banks for crabs and small fish. If a low tide comes in the early morning or late afternoon near Big Pine Key, a visit to the flats might even produce a few Key deer wading out in the shallows to feed on the leaves of scrubby red mangroves. At low tide, the islands seem more alive and isolated; it is then that they are at their most wild.

When the flood tide arrives, the life of the islands seems to sink beneath the surface of the deepening water, caught in currents that at first may be barely distinguishable, then by peak high tide feel almost like a raging torrent. The seagrass and algae bend with the tidal surge, and everything is buffeted by the rush of water flowing over the flats and through the channels. Fish, algae, seagrass, and curious snorkelers are partners in the same furious dance, swaying and rocking in an effort to maintain position against the current.

The general nature of the tides among the Keys can vary dramatically from location to location, especially since tides in the Atlantic typically have two floods and two ebbs each day, while the Gulf side may experience only one each day. The speed and direction of tidal currents can vary significantly even over short distances, which causes a real bugaboo when I try to plan photo excursions. However, currents through the main channels are consistent in that there is a nearly continuous outflow of water from the Gulf to the Atlantic. The Florida Current (an extension of

A nurse shark cruises over gorgonians on a reef. (Photo © Bill Keogh)

the Gulf Stream) then picks up this Gulf water and carries it north and east through the Florida Straits, out into the open Atlantic Ocean.

Climate

The Keys are blessed with a tropical climate that can be attributed to their southern latitude and to their being bathed in all directions by the Florida Current. The moderating effect of the surrounding warm ocean waters keeps temperatures from soaring much beyond the high eighties in the summer or dipping below the lower fifties during the winter.

Two seasons prevail in the Keys: a hot, stormy season lasting from May through October and a cooler, windy dry season lasting from November through April. April and November are months of transition and are generally ideal, with little wind and moderate temperatures. Approximately 75 percent of the Florida Keys' forty to fifty inches of annual rainfall occurs from May through October, usually in the form of daily thundershowers that rumble and flash, emptying their leaden bellies in tumultuous downpours. The storms vary in intensity, ranging from fleeting showers to violent squalls that may last two hours or more and produce waterspouts. Naturalist John James Audubon was quite impressed—terrified, actually—of an afternoon thunderstorm he weathered on a boat in the back-country during his journey through the Keys in April and May 1832. Mistaking it for a hurricane, he described the storm in his journal, ". . . now in contemplation of the sublime and awful storm, I gazed around me. The water drifted like snow; the tough mangroves hid their tops amid their roots, and the loud roaring of the waves driven among them blended with the howl of the tempest. It was not rain that fell; the masses of water flew in a horizontal direction, and where a part of my body was exposed I felt as if a smart blow had been given me on it. But enough—in half an hour it was over. The pure blue sky once more embellished the heavens. . . ."

Although Audubon never experienced an actual hurricane, tropical storms (defined as having wind speeds of 39–74 mph) and hurricanes (wind speeds greater than 74 mph) do strike the Keys on a regular basis. The peak time for hurricanes is September and October, when ocean temperatures are warmest and humidity is highest. Major damage from hurricanes results from high winds and flooding due to rainfall, storm-driven waves and tides, and storm surges. Acres of mangroves, hardwood hammocks, or pinelands may be destroyed by high winds; storm surges may send several feet of salty water over entire islands, killing freshwater vegetation and altering the soil character for years afterward; and large areas of coral may be crushed into rubble by powerful waves.

Ecosystems in the Keys, however, have coevolved with hurricanes, and many plants have developed strategies for recovering after hurricane damage. Gumbo-limbo, for example, can resprout from broken limbs lying on the hammock floor. Some naturalists think that lignum vitae, a tropical subcanopy tree, needs hurricane winds to strip away the top canopy layer of hardwood hammocks to prevent being shaded out by taller canopy species. Many tropical plants owe their very existence in the Keys to hurricanes, having been washed ashore or carried aloft by wind as seeds from the Yucatan Peninsula or West Indies. Hurricanes also appear to be a necessary ingredient in maintaining a healthy Florida Bay, especially in terms of mixing nutrient-rich waters and helping to regulate the salinity of bay waters.

Adaptations of plants and wildlife to climate

Vegetation in the Keys bears little resemblance to that of peninsular Florida, with the exception of extreme southern Florida. Most of it is tropical, tracing its origins back to hardwood forests of the Yucatan Peninsula, Central America and northern South America, Cuba and Hispaniola, and the Antilles. The Gulf Stream, hurricanes, birds, and humans are responsible for the introduction of most of the Keys' plant life.

Plants in the Keys have developed many adaptations in response to the requirements of their particular communities and to the climate in general. Soil salinity and water loss due to high heat and abundant sunlight are matters of grave concern to most species. Because the thin soil throughout the Keys does not hold much water, most plants found here have extensive, shallow root systems that allow them to benefit from rainwater immediately, before it has time to run off or percolate into the limestone. Some tropical trees such as gumbo-limbo and Jamaica dogwood are deciduous, dropping their leaves during the latter part of the dry season to conserve moisture.

Many plants are succulents, which are able to withstand arid conditions and high salt concentrations in the soil. Small, waxy leaves or thorns help prevent water loss. Salt-excretion mechanisms allow black mangroves, white mangroves, and buttonwoods to shed excess salt and survive in soils saltier than seawater. Red mangroves have adapted to a salty environment by excluding salt from entering their roots, thereby eliminating the need for salt-excretion mechanisms.

Cycles

There is a seamless connection between the past, present, and future in the development of the Keys' natural history. This is so with all ecosystems. Ecological development does not march along a one-way trail toward a future that remembers nothing of the past. Nature knows no time lines, only an endless series of cycles that continue each day, each season, each millennium. These cycles are evident all around us. Consider the ebb and flood of the tide, the progression of the seasons, the coming and going of countless generations of living things. The Keys are perched on the ancestral ecosystems that preceded them. Our islands as we know them today will eventually provide the principle foundation upon which future ecosystems will be built. The process is slow and unrelenting, but evident nonetheless. One day the sea will reclaim the Keys as its own, nurture them in its depths, and in the murky distance of eons yet to come, release them again to the light and air.

Nature knows no time lines, only an endless series of cycles that continue each day, each season, each millennium

Coral Reefs

A school of grunts patrols a reef formation.
(Photo © Bill Keogh)

I am fascinated by rainbows. Whether they appear as wisps of shimmering color in the rising

mist of a waterfall or as magnificent double arcs punctuating a dark, storming sky, I feel com-

pelled to stop and stare, gazing wide-eyed and slack-jawed at their ephemeral beauty. Fleeting

summer showers and abundant sunshine conspire to give the Keys more than their fair share of

rainbows, and as the boat in which I rode with a couple of snorkeling companions skimmed over

smooth swells on our way to Looe Key National Marine Sanctuary, the rainbow arching over the

reef against a passing shower promised a magical encounter once I slipped below the water's

surface.

An aerial view of a spur and groove reef formation, Looe Key National Marine Sanctuary. (Photo © Bill
Keogh)

RIGHT: *A bicolor damselfish guards its territory. Damselfish clear small amounts of coral to raise plots of algae on which to graze. (Photo © Bill Keogh)* BELOW: *The supermale phase of a stoplight parrotfish. (Photo © Bill Keogh)*

Coral reefs are the rainbows of the sea, the corals themselves softly glowing with shades of tan and gold, replete with bold strokes of blue and purple and pink where anemones and gorgonians have anchored themselves to coral ledges. Sunlight streams down through the water column in pale flowing veils of silver as it bathes the reef with light and intensifies the deep blue of clear ocean water pouring in from the Atlantic. The colors of coral are surpassed only by those of the creatures living in and around the reef. Drenched in hues from a wizard's neon fantasy, the names of these creatures are equally fantastic—rock beauty, queen angel, rainbow and midnight parrotfishes, yellow-headed wrasse, fairy basslet, hamlets and damselfish, blue tang, neon goby, scrawled cowfish, flamingo tongue, barber pole shrimp. Emerald-colored nurse sharks and moray eels rest under ledges and peer from crevices in the reef. At the edges of this rainbow reef, hanging motionless or finning slowly by in the blue murk of deeper water, are the sleek gray shadows of giant tarpon and barracuda.

On a calm, clear day, the deep cobalt blue of the water surrounding the fore reef mutes to pale indigo as it becomes more shallow near the reef's crest, and the rich tan color of the coral fades to nearly white at the very back edge of the reef, the rubble zone, beyond the rough and tumble of the surf. There was no surf this day—only an occasional swell that rumbled over the coral horn on the reef's west edge. As we approached the reef, I peered over the side of the boat and watched the coral fingers swirling in the clear water just below me, a liquid smear of colors set off against a pale canvas of sand. We donned snorkeling gear after tying up to one of the marine sanctuary's mooring buoys and slipped over the side of the boat, each of us bent on a personal voyage of discovery.

Swimming along the surface, I angled toward one of the several coral fingers or "spurs" that dominate the Looe Key reef formation. At the fore reef, the seaward end of the spur formation, I spied an overhang harboring a school of smallmouth grunt and other fish and dove to get a closer look. The sides of the coral rampart rose above me like a canyon wall, sea fans and sea whips gently swaying in the current as I descended toward the sandy bottom. The fish under the ledge stared at me impassively, maintaining their position even at my close approach, before I turned away to join a mixed school of blue tang and doctorfish as they swept across the coral finger. Matching my movements with theirs, we became a single mass, an indigo cloud of animal energy flowing across the reef, dipping at random to feed, and then flowing onward in a relentless surge of life. We dissolved at the edge of the reef, witnessed only by a tarpon gliding through the blue murk in the distance. I had swam with these giant tarpon before, eyeball-to-eyeball, down low among the coral canyons, breaking off contact only when they reached the edge of the fore reef on their way out to sea. Finally needing air, I shot upward, watching the sunlight streaming over the coral outcrops while the vast bowl of the sky rushed toward my face as I broke the surface. The rainbow's promise held true—the reef offered an undersea communion unlike any other experience on earth.

A first-time visitor to the reef is immediately struck by the profusion of life beneath the water's surface. The coral reef seethes with living things, layers of creatures stacked one upon the other—species upon species, generation upon generation. Space is at a premium; everything on the reef finds its place through its ability to outcompete other organisms to fill specific niches. The old and the unfit die, providing an opportunity for other animals to compete for their share of limited space and food and light.

At the core of this writhing rainbow of life is the

". . . exploring a reef is surely akin to landing on some strange planet. It is a fantastic garden, an integrated community inhabited by bizarre creatures. . . . On the reef, one can be overwhelmed with variety and profusion and the utter strangeness of it all."
—Christopher Newbert from
Within a Rainbowed Sea

reef itself, which in most cases is a coral rampart rising close to the ocean surface. This rampart is generally made up of large colonies of massive stony corals and robust branching corals crammed together, with small pieces of coral, sponge spicules, bits of shell, and other calcareous fragments filling in gaps between colonies. Only the surface layer of each colony is alive, built upon the skeletal remains of hundreds of previous generations. Chemical processes and the growth of coralline algae slowly cement the framework together, creating the coral base rock upon which the living layer of corals and red and green calcareous algae are attached. Hundreds of species of encrusting organisms also live on top of the coral framework, helping to bind the coral branches together. Fish and invertebrates dwell in nooks and crannies on the reef, while sessile organisms cover virtually every available inch of space on the underside of coral plates and dead coral skeletons.

Ecology of the coral reef

The reefs of the Florida Keys—outer bank reefs (such as the spur-and-groove formation of Looe Key) and patch reefs—are the only true living coral reefs in the continental waters of the United States. They are similar in structure and share many species with coral reefs in the Bahamas and Caribbean. Several Caribbean species reach the northernmost extent of their range in the Keys. The Florida and Caribbean reef tracts also support the richest and most diverse waving forests of sea plumes and sea whips.

Reef development is best off the major islands of the Keys chain, with the largest, most diverse bank reefs occurring on the Atlantic side off Key Largo and from Big Pine Key to Key West. The extensive land mass of these islands blocks seasonally cold water, sediments, nutrients, and other growth-inhibiting contaminants flowing through channels from Florida Bay, allowing the reefs to develop to their fullest potential. Beautiful patch reefs occur close to shore in these areas, as well as in Biscayne National Park and Dry Tortugas Na-

TOP INSET: *A spiny lobster moves over the coral near its home under a ledge on the reef. (Photo © Bill Keogh)* CENTER INSET: *A closeup view of a head of star coral. Notice the waving tentacles of individual polyps feeding on plankton. (Photo © Bill Keogh)* BOTTOM INSET: *A patch reef community. (Photo © Bill Keogh)*

ABOVE: *A Christmas tree worm on brain coral. (Photo © Bill Keogh)*

tional Park.

Bank reefs can be divided into three major zones of life. These zones are governed primarily by depth, but are also affected by wave energy and the transparency of the water. As you approach the reef from its shoreward side, you first encounter the back reef, which includes a rubble zone and reef flat comprised mainly of coralline algae, mustard hill coral, golden sea mat, bladed fire coral, green sea mat, and broken pieces of other corals swept in by wave action along the reef's seaward edge. This is a habitat of extremes, subject to heavy waves, dramatic variations in temperature, intense sunlight, and periodic tidal exposure of elevated coral outcrops. Elkhorn coral, golden sea mat, and fire coral are common on the middle zone of the reef, known as the reef crest. The fore reef is the deepest zone, boasting the most extensive coral development and harboring the greatest diversity of species, due to the greater availability of food carried by the currents. A robust branching network of elkhorn and staghorn coral dominates the shallower waters of this zone, while large buttresses of boulder coral, brain coral, star coral, and other massive stony corals occur in deeper water.

Looe Key is possibly the best example of a spur-and-groove reef system to be found in the Keys. Imagine spur-and-groove formations as submerged mountains and valleys, but on a miniature scale. The spurs are limestone formations covered with living corals. The grooves are sandy valleys between the spurs, usually no more than fourteen feet deep. The top of the shoreward end of a spur may be less than three feet deep, while the seaward end may plummet to more than thirty feet, with the entire spur formation stretching several hundred feet in length. The spur-and-groove formation usually faces into the predominant wind-sea direction and lies perpendicular to the continental shelf margin. The grooves funnel water laden with oxygen and plankton over the reef and allow sediments to pass through the coral formations with minimum damage to corals and other sessile organisms sensitive to the effects of sedimentation.

Patch reefs are found throughout much of the Keys and are the dominant reef communities found from Elliot Key to northern Key Largo. In this area alone, there are some five thousand patch reefs. Most patch reefs occur seaward of the Hawk Channel, between the channel and the bank reefs offshore. However, near Plantation Key and in the Newfound Harbor Keys, they can be found closer to shore, where they are protected from the effects of Florida Bay. Circular in shape and ranging from ten yards to several hundred yards in diameter, patch reefs generally develop on fossil reef outcrops at depths of six to thirty feet. Prominent characteristics of these reef communities are the massive heads of brain corals and sea fans and whips that rise directly from the bottom. Gorgonians cover the top of the reef. Amazingly, some patch reefs are nearly hollow inside, the underlying coral framework having been eaten away by boring clams, boring sponges, and other such termites of the sea.

Patch reefs are often surrounded by seagrass communities or sedimentary habitats. Reef-dwelling herbivorous fish venture out to graze on algae and seagrasses in these areas, creating a barren sandy "halo" that encircles the reef. The extent of the halo and its distance from the reef testifies to the bravery of the reef's inhabitants in the face of predators.

Patch reefs add diversity to the seagrass communities and often attract species from deeper water. Many of the same species that inhabit bank reefs can be found on patch reefs, together with a blending of creatures from seagrass and mangrove communities. Marine predators typically found in deeper water, such as kingfish, dolphin, and wahoo, sometimes haunt offshore patch reefs looking for easy prey.

The beauty and diversity of a coral reef make it one of nature's masterworks and are governed by a complex array of circumstances. To prosper, reef-building corals require bright sunlight; clear, warm, nutrient-free water; and relatively stable temperatures and salinity levels. The Florida Current, bringing in warm water from the Caribbean and the Gulf of Mexico, is responsible for the mild winter temperatures that permit reef development in the Florida Keys. Severe cold fronts during the winter, however, can slow growth and even kill coral on inshore reefs if water temperatures dip below sixty degrees Fahrenheit and remain there for several days.

The deep blue color and clarity of the water on coral reefs surrounding the Keys is due to the scarcity

ABOVE: *A rough fileclam on Palythoa. (Photo © Bill Keogh)*
LEFT: *A school of grunts seeks the shelter of an elkhorn coral ledge. (Photo © Bill Keogh)*

of plankton, the nutrient-rich food source so critical to teeming populations of marine life in temperate and polar waters. How then do coral reefs, considered second only to tropical rain forests in terms of biological diversity, survive in ocean surroundings so lacking in nutrients that they have been referred to as "biological deserts?" Much of the answer lies in the unique nature of the corals themselves, as well as in the relationships that have evolved among reef residents.

Corals are animals, not plants, belonging to the phylum Coelenterata, which includes sea anemones and jellyfish. The phylum's name is from the Greek *koilos*, hollow, and *enteron*, gut, because the main body cavity of its members is the digestive cavity. Hard corals or stony corals are encased by a calcareous cup and count among their members all of the reef-building corals, including the brain corals, star corals, and elkhorn and staghorn corals. Soft corals and gorgonians lack the hard, calcareous cup of hard corals and do not build reefs, although they form large colonies.

Coral generally emerge to feed only at night when what zooplankton does exist in these waters rises from the deep on a daily migration to the surface. Each individual coral animal (called a polyp) consists of three layers of cells and is basically a contractile sac crowned with a ring of six tentacles (or a multiple of six) surrounding an oral disk. Their tentacles are equipped with specialized stinging cells called nematocysts, which discharge an arrowlike barb filled with toxin for stunning prey. Food is transported in mucus along tiny, hairlike cilia that cover the polyp and beat it toward the mouth. Some corals can't wait for the cilia to do their job and speed along the transport of food to

the stomach by wiping their tentacles across their mouths.

Because the water on the reef is so low in nutrients, many corals rely on other living marine organisms to help supplement their food supply. Zooxanthellae are microscopic algae that live in the tissues of several species of stony corals. Their name originates from "zoo," meaning animal, and "xanth," meaning gold, referring to their yellowish-brown color. In some cases, zooxanthellae in the coral tissues are what give the coral colonies their brilliant hues.

The relationship between the coral polyps and zooxanthellae is considered a mutualistic relationship, a form of symbiosis in which both the algae and the coral benefit from the arrangement. Algae, being plants, conduct photosynthesis, thereby producing food and oxygen that are consumed by the coral polyp. The algae obtain shelter and waste products (primarily carbon dioxide and nitrogen) from the coral. Zooxanthellae also contribute to the ability of hard corals to produce calcium carbonate, the primary reef-building material of stony corals. Carbon dioxide and water are by-products of animal metabolism and will dissolve or significantly slow down the deposition of calcium carbonate spicules that make up the coral skeletons. As zooxanthellae conduct photosynthesis, they remove excess water and carbon dioxide, thereby reducing the acidity inside the polyp and enhancing its ability to construct its skeleton.

This cooperation between coral and zooxanthellae is so important that neither organism can survive well without the other. In some corals, as much as half of each polyp's weight consists of zooxanthellae.

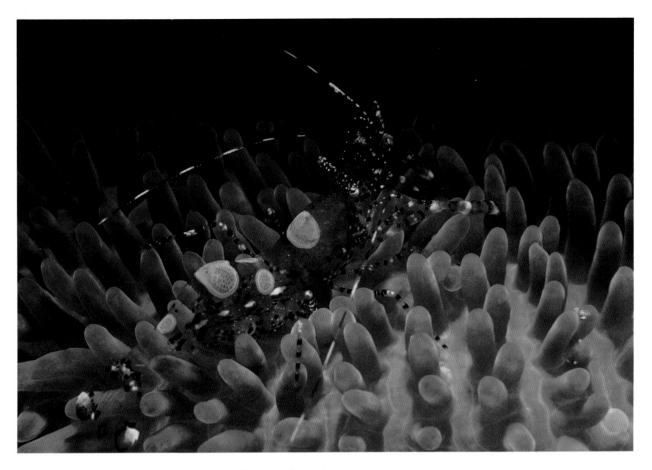

A spotted cleaner shrimp on a sun anemone. (Photo © Bill Keogh)

Certainly reefs would not exist without the coral-zooxanthellae relationship because only corals containing zooxanthellae can maintain the high metabolism and ability to produce the large quantities of calcium carbonate required for reef development.

Corals reproduce sexually and asexually. Once a coral animal is fertilized, the planulae (larval coral) develop inside the adult until they are large enough to be released to take their chances in the open sea. Some corals release their young only once a year; others release planulae all year long. As planulae are released, they swim upwards toward the light, using hundreds of hairlike cilia to propel themselves through the water, where they become part of the microscopic stream of planktonic life that swarms near the surface. Some planulae are caught up in the Gulf Stream that sweeps them as far north as Bermuda, contributing to the development of the magnificent reefs in that area. Almost all planulae, however, are eaten by reef creatures within a few hours of being released. Those that sur-

vive the rigors of their planktonic existence reverse themselves within several days and head toward the bottom to become polyps. With luck, they settle on a hard, clean, silt-free surface, each polyp endowed with the potential to become a new colony through asexual budding. Once a polyp settles, it cannot move again. Polyps that do not settle on a suitable growing surface soon die.

Some corals, such as depressed brain coral, common rose coral, and star coral, are hermaphroditic, meaning that they produce both sperm and eggs at the same time. Although self-fertilization in these species is possible, it almost never occurs because cross-fertilization among different polyps ensures that offspring with a variety of characteristics are produced, enabling the coral colony as a whole to better cope with environmental changes.

Asexual reproduction occurs primarily by budding. Budding is a process in which a polyp divides itself to form another polyp, which in turn divides to form still another polyp, each with its own calcareous cup. The budding process and skeleton construction continue until the final coral colony, as we know it, is formed. Another form of asexual reproduction is fragmentation, whereby if a living coral colony is broken off or fragmented by a storm or boat grounding, new colonies may form from the broken pieces and attach themselves to the bottom if they are left undisturbed and if growing conditions are favorable.

Growth rates differ markedly among different species of coral. Branching corals such as elkhorn and staghorn corals grow rapidly, adding as much as four inches a year, with most of the growth occurring at the tips. On the other hand, massive stony corals such as star and brain corals grow upward and outward, adding as little as one-half inch per year.

The overall growth of the reef is the result of a dynamic relationship between the upward extension of the coral reef and the flushing away and erosion of a much larger volume of fine-grained detritus. Unstable piles of coral may also grow until they topple under their own weight, rolling down to the foot of the reef base. If the water is clear and shallow enough, there may be ample light for the coral to continue growing, providing an extension to the living reef.

Coral maturation is a slow process as well. Most stony corals take several years to reach sexual maturity. Slow-growing massive stony corals such as brain corals may take up to eight years to mature, while faster-growing branching species such as elkhorn coral mature somewhat more quickly.

Because so many corals grow and mature so slowly, damage caused by predators, storms, and humans can cause a reef to deteriorate rapidly. Recovery takes decades; estimates for the time it takes for a reef to rebound from damage caused by a severe storm range from twenty to fifty years. Although certain species of coral may become quite common within ten to twenty years, a reef is not considered to be fully recovered until its original diversity of slow-growing massive coral species and faster-growing branching species has returned to normal. Recovery to this level may take a century or longer.

Reefs are constantly being torn down and built up by a variety of ecological processes. Bio-erosion is the term used by ecologists to describe the biologically caused tearing-down process of a reef. Many species of filamentous algae, fungi, sponges, sea worms, crustaceans, and mollusks bore into coral skeletons, excavating holes by mechanical rasping or chemical dissolution. One of the most common bio-eroders is the boring sponge *Cliona*, which chips out tiny pieces of calcium carbonate at a rate of more than three feet every seventy years. Damselfish and other herbivorous fish may destroy small amounts of living coral when they clear patches to farm their plots of algae. The damselfish, which graze on the algae, defend their plots vigorously and chase any intruders on their territory, including larger fish and curious divers.

Parrotfish are prodigious coral munchers. Studies have shown that for every acre of reef, parrotfish have converted nearly one ton of solid coral skeleton to a fine sand as they graze algae from the reef. When snorkeling or diving near a feeding parrotfish, you can actually hear it biting off chunks of coral with its hard, beak-shaped mouth. The coral skeleton is pulverized into sand with grinding plates in the fish's throat, the nutrients (from algae and incidentally taken coral polyps) being assimilated and the waste passing from the fish to fall to the ocean floor.

You can actually hear a parrotfish biting off chunks of coral with its hard, beak-shaped mouth

Most of the parrotfish's feeding on living coral results in spotty damage, with bare white areas occurring here and there on the surface of a coral head. Damage of this nature can usually be repaired by the coral within two to three months.

Coral-eating reef residents play a significant role in the shaping of a reef, but their actions in general should not be viewed as detrimental. Instead, they are quite necessary. Pitting and undercutting caused by bio-erosion increases a reef's surface area, providing additional habitat that can be used as attachment sites for corals, anemones, tunicates, bryozoans, and sponges.

Coral polyps are subject to injury from a host of

OVERLEAF: *A gray angelfish, a large, distinctive reef dweller that eats sponges. (Photo © Bill Keogh)*

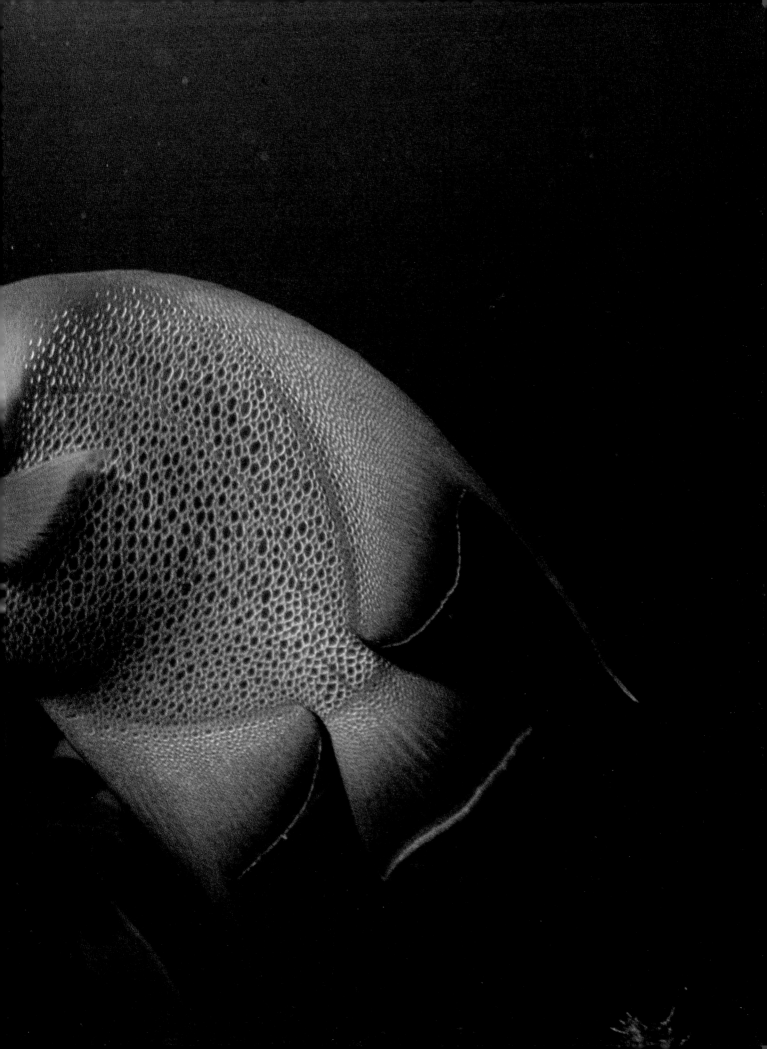

A green moray eel venturing out of its hole. (Photo © Bill Keogh)

environmental factors other than direct predation and bio-erosion. A small area of damaged reef is like an open wound, exposing the rest of the colony to attack by bacteria, fungi, and algae, which can quickly overgrow bare spots and weakened polyps. During the summer, water temperatures may soar to over 90 degrees on shallow, partially exposed reefs, causing coral polyps to expel their zooxanthellae and potentially dooming them to death by starvation. Suspended sediments, pollutants, and excess nutrients can cause polyps to produce too much mucus, spurring rapid bacterial growth and causing stressful conditions for the coral. Plankton, suspended organic matter, and sediments diminish water clarity, thereby reducing the amount of sunlight available to zooxanthellae for conducting photosynthesis. As a result, less energy is generated and coral growth slows.

Competition for light and space among corals is intense. Fast-growing species overshadow slower-growing corals by blocking light and water flow to understory colonies. Other corals, such as fire coral, colonize living octocoral branches. Some corals digest the tissues of neighboring polyps of a different species through the extension of mesenterial filaments, which are special digestive tubes attached to the stomach. Other corals counter these attacks through a variety of chemical defenses and offenses. The struggle for life is passionate even in a habitat seemingly as tranquil and beautiful as the coral reef.

One of my favorite things to do on a snorkeling trip to the reef is to look for spiny lobsters. Spiny lobsters, also known as crawfish or "bugs," are possibly the single most sought-after resident on the reef. Commercial lobster season lasts from August through

spined carapace is yellow or cream and reddish brown, with two black and white horns located on the top of the head like arched eyebrows. The legs are lined in yellow or cream, while the abdomen is peppered with whitish spots. The long antennae are reddish brown and can be folded back along the entire length of the body.

Spiny lobsters are nocturnal feeders, preying mainly on snails and clams. They also eat worms, crabs, shrimp, sea urchins, sponges, and small fish. In turn, the lobsters are preyed upon by snappers, sharks, rays, octopi, groupers, nurse sharks, and of course, humans. Florida lobsters lack the claws of their cousins from Maine, defending themselves instead by vigorously flapping their spiny tails against attackers. They may also rattle their antennae when threatened to alert other lobsters in the area that there is danger.

Breeding season for spiny lobsters lasts from March through July. When spiny lobsters mate, they lie face to face, the male leaving a patch of sticky fluid filled with sperm on the female's belly. This spot, which hardens into a black patch, is called a "tar spot" and is

March, but a July two-day "mini-season" gives sport divers a first crack at catching their limit. I am not overly fond of lobster in the pot, but I enjoy looking at them in their holes. You can quickly find a lobster by keeping a sharp eye out for a pair of long, segmented antennae waving in the current, usually from inside a dark hole or beneath a deep recess in the reef. If you rub a lobster's antenna, it may come out to investigate, but most individuals retreat quickly into their caves.

Although sometimes rather drab, most spiny lobsters are beautifully colored. The cylindrical, sharply

a good indication that a female lobster will soon lay eggs. Once the female lays her eggs, she carries them beneath her tail, fertilizing them by scraping the tar spot with the spurs on her last set of legs. A female carrying eggs is called a "berried" lobster because the eggs resemble thousands of bright orange berries. The female will carry her eggs for one to four weeks, protecting them from predators and fanning them with water to keep them well-oxygenated. When they are ready to hatch, the eggs turn from bright orange to dark brown.

Once lobster larvae hatch, they spend at least six months floating in the plankton stream. They look nothing like the adults, having flat, clear bodies and long, thin legs. After their planktonic stage, they metamorphose into baby lobsters that are minute, transparent replicas of the adults. These young lobsters can swim, and they head for the protection of mangrove swamps and seagrass beds. There they lose their transparency and turn pale yellow with dark brown banding. As juvenile lobsters mature, they move from the inshore areas to patch reefs before finally heading for the deeper reefs to breed.

Most lobsters begin to mate when they are between three and five years old (about eight to ten inches long). If a lobster's back is more than three-and-a-half inches long, it is about three years old and probably ready to mate. Spiny lobsters can live to nearly twenty-five years of age and reach more than two feet in length from head to tail.

Like all arthropods, spiny lobsters have a hard outer skin (exoskeleton), which they periodically outgrow. The old skin is shed by molting. When a lobster molts, the old shell splits where the body joins the tail, and the lobster backs out of the shell from this opening. The soft new shell that has developed under the old one swells to a larger size and gradually hardens. The lobster now has room to grow until it is once again time to molt.

On several occasions, I have been overwhelmed by the sheer size of some of the creatures I have encountered on the reef during a snorkeling trip. Once,

On several occasions, I have been overwhelmed by the sheer size of some of the creatures I have encountered on the reef

an immense brain coral formation at Looe Key struck me as being particularly impressive. On another trip, it was a massive six-foot barracuda that resembled a naval battle cruiser more than a fish. Another time, two huge supermale (or terminal-phase male) rainbow parrotfish, each the size of a coral boulder, cruised into the shallow water where a friend and I were looking for flamingo tongues on sea fans. These parrotfish were giants among parrotfish, even for supermales.

The entire biological concept of supermales among parrotfish, wrasses, and several other reef fishes is a fascinating phenomenon in and of itself. Not only are supermales much larger than other members of the species, they are often much more brightly colored and display habits remarkably different from the rest of the population. Parrotfish are one of several families of coral reef fish that are sequential hermaphrodites, undergoing a hormonally induced functional sex-reversal at some point in life. Most species of parrotfish are dimorphic, consisting of two distinct color and size forms (phases) of individuals. Relatively small, drab-colored individuals are the initial-phase group and comprise mainly females, although males are present. Larger, brightly colored fish are termphase fish or supermales, which at some point are produced from a given population of initial-phase males and females. In many species, supermales are territorial and dominate harems of initial-phase females. What causes an initial-phase male or female to become a supermale? No one knows for sure, although environmental factors and population dynamics may be determining factors.

A crucial aspect of life on a reef is the ability of individual species to fit within extremely specific niches in the ecosystem through an incredible array of different feeding strategies. One such strategy is to feed in shifts. For example, squirrelfish are nocturnal feeders, while wrasses are diurnal or daytime feeders. Both of these small fish dine on shrimp, crustaceans, and worms. By feeding at different times of the day, they avoid directly competing with each other for the same

ouflage and stealth to snatch prey. Trumpetfish and coronetfish are long, thin fish that are nearly indistinguishable from the soft corals you find them near. These fish hang vertically among the corals, camouflaged by their dark colors and vertical striping, drifting slowly until they are close enough to suck small prey into their tiny mouths. Ambush predators such as the lizardfish and scorpionfish rely on camouflage as well, but have evolved one step further. Unlike most other fish, they have no swim bladder, a physiological adaptation that helps them to stay near the ocean floor, and their mouths face upwards to allow them to snatch prey while lying in wait in the sand or on rocks.

food source. Only rarely do you find daytime feeders and nocturnal feeders together. Nocturnal feeders generally come out only when the daytimers have retired to their crevices and ledges for the evening.

Some fish have evolved as predators, while others have become herbivores. Predators are most active at dawn and dusk, when the greatest numbers of prey are moving to and from feeding grounds and resting places. Easily recognizable predators on the reef include barracuda, snappers, groupers, grunts, tarpon, and sharks.

Less obvious predators are those that rely on cam-

Some fish eat creatures that most other sea life find disgusting. French, gray, and queen angelfish rely on sponges for food. Sponges are typically foul tasting, and have a bad odor, sharp spicules, and toxins in their tissues. However, these fish have evolved to overcome these defenses and take advantage of a food source used by few other creatures.

Perhaps the most remarkable survival strategies,

however, are those that involve symbiotic relationships. A symbiotic relationship in its most general sense is a relationship from which both organisms benefit in some way. Consider the star-eyed hermit, which carries around anemones on the snail shell in which it lives. The stinging tentacles of the anemones provide the crab with protection against predators, while the anemones are believed to benefit by being transported on the crab to food sources they would not ordinarily be able to exploit. Studies documenting the reactions of octopi to hermit crabs (the star-eyed hermit is a favorite dish of the common Atlantic octopus) with and without anemones showed that crabs attacked by octopi always survived when they had an anemone partner, while those crabs without anemones were always killed in an attack.

Commensalism is a type of symbiotic relationship in which one creature benefits from a common food supply while the other one is not adversely affected. A commensal relationship exists between the gall crab and elkhorn coral. The gall crab settles on a branch of elkhorn or staghorn coral as a juvenile resembling a tiny lobster. The coral's skeleton grows around the crab to form a gall about the size of a dime. The crab is not restricted to the gall and can move around freely. Abandoned galls are readily occupied by other gall crabs searching for new homes. Bar jacks, probably the most common species of jack found on the reef, sometimes form a commensal relationship with Spanish hogfish, picking up scraps from the hogfish's meal. When a jack feeds this way, it changes from its normal silvery hue to a medium brown color.

Divers and snorkelers who frequently visit reefs more than likely have witnessed a cleaning station in action. Cleaning stations are specific points on the reef where a crowd of fish may gather and line up to obtain the services of certain small fish and crustaceans (called cleaners) present at the station. Cleaners feed on irritating parasites or damaged tissues of the skin, mouth, and gills of fish found in inshore areas of the Keys, as well as other species that come in from deeper water. Both cleaners and the host fish often assume unusual postures or perform rituals to initialize and

A combination of natural and human-caused conditions is wiping out entire stands of corals over the course of months, weeks, and even days

maintain the cleaning interaction. Some fish stand on their heads or tails. Others yawn, flaring their gills and fins. Cleaners are usually distinctively marked and frequently perform a "cleaner dance" to identify themselves as cleaners and to indicate their willingness to begin cleaning. Cleaners found on reefs in the Keys and elsewhere in the Caribbean include the sharknose goby, several wrasses (such as the Spanish hogfish and slippery dick wrasse), yellowtail damselfish, spotted cleaning shrimp, banded coral (barber pole) shrimp, and peppermint shrimp.

Threats to the coral reef

The coral reefs of the Florida Keys are an ecosystem in distress. A combination of natural and human-caused conditions is wiping out entire stands of corals over the course of months, weeks, and even days. The coral reefs of the Keys are already at a disadvantage because they are located at the northern boundary of their range in the Caribbean. Severe cold fronts sometimes bring water temperatures down to levels below those which the coral can easily withstand. Another blow comes from Florida Bay, a critical situation some scientists have referred to as "being stabbed in the back by your own lagoon." Since the formation of Florida Bay, coral reefs in the Keys have maintained a delicate equilibrium with tidal water flowing from the Bay. Depending on the season, this bay water is rapidly chilled or heated, diluted by fresh water, or made more salty through evaporation—deadly ingredients for a coral ecosystem dependent on consistent environmental conditions.

The situation with Florida Bay has deteriorated still further. Intense agriculture and urban development have eaten away at the Everglades, the giant marshy system lying to the north of Florida Bay and the Keys. Thousands of acres have been developed, and much of the water that once flowed from the Kissimmee River through Lake Okeechobee and the Everglades to Florida Bay has been diverted for human use. Florida Bay no longer receives the seasonal influx of fresh water it once did, and what water it does receive is tainted with pesticides, heavy metals, and excessive loads of nutrients. Parts of the bay have become twice as salty as seawater and subject to immense algae blooms. A large area of the bay is devoid of fish life, prompting fishermen to dub it "the dead zone," and since 1987 die-offs of tens of thousands of acres of seagrass beds have robbed Florida Bay of important habitat and precious filtering abilities. In short, the water flowing from Florida Bay into Hawk Channel and throughout the Florida reef tract may be lethal to coral reefs over the long term.

The coral reef's water woes don't end with Florida Bay. Human effluent is pumped into porous limestone throughout the Keys every day. This waste eventually makes its way out to the reefs, increasing nutrients in the seawater bathing the reefs to levels that promote the growth of algae, not coral. Now factor in visits from thousands of divers every day to the Keys' most popular reef destinations, such as John Pennekamp Coral Reef State Park and Looe Key National Marine Sanctuary. Nearly one million people visit the reefs of Key Largo National Marine Sanctuary each year, and some 75,000 people visit Looe Key each year. Despite informational brochures and lectures from sanctuary officers, dive shop operators, and snorkeling and diving concession services regarding the use of mooring buoys and how to safely snorkel or dive on the reef, coral gets touched, anchors occasionally break off coral heads, and boats ground. The overall effect of this formidable array of natural and human-caused problems is that the coral is dying faster than it can replace itself. If conditions do not improve, the entire coral reef ecosystem will be in danger of collapse.

Proper reef etiquette

When visiting a coral reef, you will undoubtedly receive a brochure, view a slide show, or see signs informing you of how to properly experience the reef without damaging it. These guidelines summarize some of the most important points to keep in mind:

1) Before booking a reef trip, check weather conditions. Rough seas, strong winds, and poor visibility are not conducive to a safe and enjoyable outing.

2) Use reef mooring buoys or anchor in sandy areas away from coral to avoid damaging coral or seagrass beds with an anchor and chain.

3) Wear float-vests when snorkeling so that you can adjust your gear without standing on coral. When diving, practice proper buoyancy control and avoid using too much weight so that you will stay off the ocean floor. Seemingly lifeless areas may support new growth if left undisturbed.

4) Avoid wearing gloves or touching marine life. You may scrape off the thin living layer of coral from its base before you realize it.

5) Never stand on or break off coral. Try to avoid kicking up sand around coral or sponges. The clouds of sand blanket these animals and inhibit their ability to feed.

6) Don't feed the fish. It disrupts their natural feeding patterns and may leave them more susceptible to spear fishing or collecting.

7) It is illegal to collect coral in Florida, and buying it in local shops only depletes reefs elsewhere.

8) Dumping trash at sea is illegal. Plastic bags, plastic six-pack rings, monofilament, and other debris kill marine animals and birds. Try to retrieve old nets, fishing line, or other fishing debris when you encounter them.

The coral reefs of the Florida Keys are a unique world treasure—beautiful, delicate, dynamic, yet incapable of surmounting all of the challenges that now face them. The wrath of hurricanes, the flow of currents from Florida Bay to the Atlantic—these are events that have progressed over several thousand years, events over which we have no control. But we *are* guilty for much of what is killing the reefs, and we *must* take responsibility for our actions. The rehabilitation of Florida Bay, better sewage treatment, fewer pesticide applications for mosquito control, more emphasis on educating divers and snorkelers about coral reefs—these are things we can do in the name of coral reef preservation. Rachel Carson wrote about Florida's coral reefs in *The Edge of the Sea*: "And offshore, under the surface waters where the moonlight falls in broken, argent beams, under the tidal currents streaming shoreward in the still night, the pulse of life surges on the reef." Now is the time to ensure that the pulse of life on the reef is not stilled forever.

Nearshore Environments

Turtle grass with a host of epiphytic organisms attached to the surface of the blades.
(Photo © Bill Keogh)

Canoe travel is one of my favorite means for getting around in the backcountry of the Keys. On calm days, I can solo paddle, and on days when the breeze makes paddling alone difficult, I'll take a friend. Early one afternoon, I set out in my fourteen-foot Mohawk with a companion on a short trip to Howe and Annette Keys, two backcountry islands to the north and west of Big Pine Key. Our main purpose was to photograph sharks at Annette Key and then, if we had time, catch the late afternoon light and sunset at Howe Key before paddling back. With a fifteen-knot breeze from the southeast at our backs, we jetted across the narrow bay separating Big Pine from Annette and Mayo Keys. Once we crossed the bay, we hugged the shoreline close to the mangroves,

A bed of turtle grass stretches toward a distant mangrove island, National Key Deer Refuge. (Photo © Jeff Ripple)

RIGHT: *Sponge on an algal flat. (Photo © Jeff Ripple)* BELOW: *A dolphin surfaces to breathe at sunset, National Key Deer Refuge. (Photo © Bill Keogh)*

where we would be protected from the wind. The breeze kept mosquitoes back in the interior of the island, allowing us to explore the numerous cuts and passages along the mangrove perimeter. Lemon and nurse sharks nosed up to the bank under mangroves, especially in areas with a firm, sandy bottom and little algae. After an hour at Annette, we struck out toward the limestone flats on the west side of Howe Key. Small sharks were there as well, frequently gliding between us as we waded the flats among the stubby little mangroves that dotted the west shore. Finally, just after the sun slipped below the horizon into the Gulf, we loaded up the canoe and dug our paddles in against the breeze for the trip back to Big Pine Key.

Darkness comes quickly to the Keys once the sun has set. With the afterglow to our backs, we pitched and rocked around the north tip of Big Pine Key, crossing the shallow flats on the receding tide. Suddenly, a tremendous swirl buffeted the canoe and as we turned to look behind us, a huge shark erupted from the surface, silhouetted against a flame-red sky. The behe-

moth flung itself almost entirely clear of the water before falling back not more than twenty feet from the canoe's stern. The shark must have spooked after we passed over it in the grassy shallows in the dim light. Several minutes passed before we were able to pick ourselves off the floor of the canoe and resume paddling. By then, what little light remained in the western sky had faded, and we were immersed in complete darkness as we continued our journey across the flats. Needless to say, with nerves on edge for the remainder of the trip, we jumped at even small splashes close to the canoe.

A giant anemone at the base of a loggerhead sponge. (Photo © Bill Keogh)

The night, however, was still filled with surprises for us. As we crossed certain areas of the flats, our paddles stirred up hundreds of bioluminescent creatures from the seagrass and hardbottom, creating a swirling, sparkling universe with each stroke. Some of the creatures twinkled on the surface like reflections of stars, but most eddied up from the bottom. In the distance to the north, lightning illuminated the towering anvilheads of several thunderstorms over Florida Bay. More stars than I had ever seen before whirled overhead as we pressed forward into the stiff wind and heavy chop that now separated us from the boat ramp where we had launched earlier in the day. This trip was not my first experience with the backcountry flats of the Keys, but it was certainly among the most memorable.

The flats are part of what are considered by naturalists to be the nearshore habitats of the Keys. Most flats contain either seagrass meadows or hardbottom communities. They are the favorite haunts of fishermen searching for tarpon, permit, bonefish, and other game fish common in these areas. They are also fascinating places to snorkel or wade.

More stars than I had ever seen before whirled overhead as we pressed forward into the stiff wind and heavy chop

As prolific as life is in these shallow waters, survival is not easy. Plants and animals living here must cope with a formidable array of environmental fluctuations. Air temperature and sunlight can dramatically raise or drop water temperatures. Rain, storm runoff, and evaporation can change salinities in restricted bays and channels. Wind and tidal changes can stir up sediments, thereby reducing water clarity, which in turn restricts the amount of sunlight penetrating the water column for plant photosynthesis.

Seagrass beds are the most common habitat in shallow waters landward from the reef and in protected bays in the backcountry. They, like mangroves, are extremely productive ecosystems that contribute heavily to the overall health of the integrated Keys environment. Manatee grass, shoal grass, and turtle grass are the three major types of flowering underwater grasses in the Keys. Manatee grass can be easily identified by its rounded blades, while shoal grass and turtle grass have flat blades. Turtle grass has the widest blades of the three species.

Manatee grass and shoal grass are ephemeral grasses found growing in the soft, sandy bottom. They are especially important as pioneers, creating suitable sites on which extensive beds of turtle grass may later develop. It is in the turtle grass beds that most of the nutrients produced by mangroves and upland systems are trapped and used. The long, flat, wide blades, which often exceed a foot in length and one-quarter to three-quarters of an inch in width, offer plenty of surface area for marine organisms to attach themselves. Dense root systems extend more than two feet into the sand, preventing it from eroding away. The grass grows in extensive beds, providing shelter and a vast food supply for shrimp, spiny lobsters, crabs, and dozens of kinds of fish, including familiar species such as mangrove snapper, sea trout, permit, barracuda, grunt, and parrotfish.

Turtle grass provides more than just food and housing for marine life. It also plays a critical role in preventing ocean-bound sediments from reaching the coral reef. As sediment-laden water passes over the grass beds, the sediments slowly sink among the leaves and to the bottom. Only heavy wave action or turbulence from boat propellers stirs them up, placing them back into suspension. It is largely because of surrounding turtle grass beds that the water clarity is maintained around patch reefs, permitting stony corals to prosper with the aid of their zooxanthellae.

Unfortunately, seagrass beds are dwindling at an astonishing rate in Florida Bay and the Keys. One of the most significant problems facing these beds is damage caused by boat groundings and propeller scarring. To protect shallow-water habitat, some state and federally protected areas in the backcountry prohibit the use of powerboats. For example, in the Lignumvitae Key State Aquatic Preserve, a 10,000-acre reserve comprised primarily of nearshore seagrass beds and hardbottom that falls under the management of Lignumvitae Key State Botanical Site, park officials proposed "noncombustion zones" for areas in three feet of water or less. This designation would allow boaters to use an electric motor or to pole across the shal-

ABOVE: *Sharks, such as this nurse shark, are frequently seen swimming on the flats in search of food. (Photo © Jeff Ripple)*
LEFT: *Pipefish among fragments of seagrasses and mixed algae. (Photo © Bill Keogh)*

low flats, but they would not be allowed to use an engine. A channel marking program was also introduced in an effort to reduce the number of groundings in areas where channels are not well-defined. According to Pat Wells, manager of Lignumvitae Key State Botanical Site, in a three-week period there may be as many as twelve groundings or serious prop-dredging incidents. The new programs would protect fragile nearshore habitat, while at the same time prevent boaters from damaging their boats in grounding incidents and from incurring fines to mitigate the environmental damage caused by their groundings.

Another major problem affecting seagrass beds lies to the north of the Keys in the Everglades. The drastic reduction of fresh water from the Everglades has caused an enormous increase in the salinity of Florida Bay, particularly during the dry season. This is believed to have contributed significantly to the die-off of vast areas of seagrass in Florida Bay.

Hardbottom communities

Hardbottom habitat is a shallow-water system characterized by exposed or thinly covered bedrock or cemented (fossilized) sediment and rubble. Hardbottom communities are dominated by algae, sponges, soft corals, and ahermatypic stony corals, all of which attach themselves to the bedrock. Algae is most often thought of as a slimy green mass that covers freshwater ponds and lakes, but in the Keys, many species of algae are delicately shaped and are actually quite captivating. Seabottle, star algae, green bubble algae, and mermaid's wineglass are only a few of these species that resemble green vessels of finely blown glass more than plants.

Soft corals found on hardbottom include knobby and spiny candelabra, sea fans, double-forked sea rods, dry sea plume, gray sea rod, and slimy sea plume. Ahermatypic stony corals (which have developed a mucous system that can withstand the high suspended sediment load in shallow waters) include smooth starlet coral, golf ball coral, bifurcate finger coral, mustard hill coral, rose coral, elliptical star coral, knobby brain coral, and smooth brain coral. Anemones,

conchs and tulip snails, spider and stone crabs, sea stars, sea cucumbers, and tunicates are common, as are juvenile spiny lobsters in crevices. Grunt, snapper, small grouper, and barracuda, needlefish, and occasionally tarpon haunt these communities.

Sponges

Hardbottom areas in the Keys provide ideal conditions for loggerhead, stinker, sprawling, vase, chicken liver, and fire sponges. Sponges are virtual condominiums for tiny sea creatures, frequently housing thousands of pistol shrimp, gobies, and worms. Sponges, members of the phylum Porifera, are the most primitive of multicelled animals in that they consist of only a few kinds of cells arranged in layers. These evolutionary dead-ends are considered a link between colonies of one-celled creatures and all other true multicelled animals; no other higher animals have evolved from sponges. Nonetheless, they are fascinating in their own right and are essential members of coral reefs and the nearshore community.

A typical sponge has an outer skin and a central mass riddled with chambers lined with special cells called choanocytes. The choanocytes filter plankton, bacteria, and other microscopic particles out of the water as it passes through the inner chambers.

Sponges are essential members of coral reefs and the nearshore community

The water then enters a series of exhaust canals that fuse into one large cavity that opens to the outside water through a large hole called the osculum. From more than three feet away, a snorkeler hanging above a large sponge can feel a current of water being expelled through the osculum. Most sponges have an inner skeleton of rigid needles called spicules. The spicules, which look like tiny slivers of glass, are often interwoven with a tough, fibrous material called spongin. The network of spicules and spongin create a tough, rubbery framework strong enough to support giant sponges, such as barrel sponges and loggerhead sponges. Other sponges, such as the fire sponge and chicken liver sponge, encrust any solid object they

A corkscrew anemone on an algal flat. (Photo © Bill Keogh)

encounter and take on its shape.

A variety of fish, shrimp, crabs, clams, colonial anemones, brittle stars, tunicates, flatworms, and other creatures live in the nooks, crannies, and internal cavities of sponges. Pistol shrimp are among the most common shrimp found in sponges; thousands of them may inhabit a large loggerhead sponge. Some pistol shrimp spend their entire adult lives within the crevices of a sponge, never venturing beyond the safety of its inner cavities.

Besides their use as bath sponges, sponges are harvested for medicinal uses. The fire sponge alone has yielded eight antibiotics, while other species are known to produce substances with bacteria-killing or cancer-inhibiting properties. Although the present demand for natural sponges does not approach that of the past, it is sufficient to support a small commercial sponge-fishing industry.

Other nearshore systems

Hardbottom and seagrass beds cover most of the nearshore areas in the Keys, but other systems exist here as well. Sand and mud habitats, covering much of the bottom between the reef and the shoreline, are formed by loose white sand originating from the skeletons of marine plants and animals. Mud bottom supports a variety of erect green algae, clams, snails, worms, and echinoids. Burrowing *Callianassa* shrimp make conical mounds in this mud, often forming what resemble little undersea villages in backcountry shallows in and around seagrass beds.

The White Banks off Key Largo, the area shoreward of the reef at Looe Key, and the bare sandy valleys that occur between the coral fingers of spur-and-groove reefs are representative of the sand habitats of the Keys. Here you find the erect shaving brush algae, sea urchins, clams, and worms.

The queen conch

Among the most celebrated residents of nearshore seagrass communities is the queen conch, symbol of the Florida Keys. This snail is probably one of the most popular seashells in the world because of its large, heavy shell with the characteristic pink, flaring lip. It is found throughout the Keys, the Bahamas, and the Caribbean, ranging as far north as south Florida and Bermuda. The snail prefers firm, sandy bottom with rock or seagrass beds in water depths ranging from the shallows near shoreline to more than four hundred feet. It is a vegetarian, preferring soft marine algae and bacterial debris.

Queen conchs mate from February through October. Females lay eggs about three weeks after mating and produce six to seven egg masses per season. Nearly 500,000 eggs are encased in a crescent-shaped egg mass resembling a wad of sandy, cooked spaghetti noodles. In three to five days, the eggs hatch into veligers, tiny conch larvae that bear no resemblance to the adults. The veligers join other zooplankton drifting in the currents and feed on single-celled plants in the water column. In four weeks, those veligers that have survived the rigors of planktonic life settle to the bottom and metamorphose into bottom-dwelling snails no larger than a grain of sand. Young snails hide in the sand and among seagrass for their first year, eluding fish, crabs, lobsters, octopi, and loggerhead turtles. In about three years, they will reach their full size of nine to ten inches. In spite of their formidable shell, even adult queen conchs are faced with many predators, including loggerhead turtles, octopi, nurse sharks, stingrays, and a few predatory snails. Humans are their greatest threat, killing more conchs than all other predators combined.

Among the most celebrated residents of nearshore seagrass communities is the queen conch, symbol of the Florida Keys

Conchs become sexually mature at four years of age and generally live to be about seven, although older snails have been recorded. An adult snail can be distinguished from a juvenile by its distinctive, glossy, pink flared lip. Juveniles are mottled brown and white when they are about two inches long, and as they grow, the shell becomes a uniform tan outside with a yellowish-pink inside and a straight lip. Old conchs tend to have worn shells with a dark, thick lip that has lost most of the flare.

Historically, conch meat was a daily staple in the Keys, harvested while wading with a hooked staff and water glass (an instrument consisting of an open box or tube with a glass bottom used to examine submerged objects). The snails were so plentiful that they could be gathered by the armload from the shallow waters in which they thrived. This changed in the 1960s when advanced technology and an insatiable commercial demand for the shells in tourist shops and the meat in chowders and fritters nearly wiped them out. By 1985, hardly any queen conchs were left, and all taking of conch was prohibited as a last-ditch effort to save the species in the Keys. Today, conch meat and shells are imported from other countries in the Caribbean. Queen conch is protected in state and federal waters, and as a result, the population in the Keys appears to be on the upswing once again. Like all creatures in the Keys, however, the future of the queen conch is dependent on the preservation of its environment. Whether its comeback can continue will be in part contingent on how well we protect nearshore habitats. If we fail in this mission, we stand to lose more than just another species; we will have lost the very symbol of the Florida Keys itself.

Mangroves

*A red mangrove at low tide shows lichen growth and
the distinctive arching structure of its roots.*
(Photo © Jeff Ripple)

Two broad strokes with the canoe blade pushed me away from the boat ramp off U.S. 1 into the still, gray waters of Little Blackwater Sound in Everglades National Park. A faint breeze freshened from the southwest, dissipating the remnants of the previous evening's thunderstorms. Clear sky in that direction promised no rain at least through the morning. After twenty minutes of paddling, the sounds of the road finally faded into the thick air, and I was wrapped in a wilderness of mangroves. The ascending trills of a palm warbler filtered out from somewhere among the fleshy leaves and arching roots of the trees, and a red-winged blackbird belted out its musical call as a counterpoint to the low, guttural cooing of a white-crowned pigeon. Other than the

Mangrove crabs are frequently found clinging to the roots of red mangroves. (Photo © Bill Keogh)

voices of these few birds, there were few sounds besides those of my paddle blade entering the water and the gurgle of the canoe's wake. I was mesmerized by the solitude.

Although the forest can seem eerily silent, the hush is never complete. Sometimes the calm is broken by the slap of a shark's tail as it moves through a narrow tidal channel or by the low hum of mosquitoes swarming within the tangle of leaves and branches. At other times the forest is raucous, trees literally shaking with the heavy flapping and deafening calls of multitudes of cormorants, frigatebirds, egrets, herons, and brown pelicans vying for space to roost or nest.

In the mangrove forests I have explored along the southwest coast of Florida, the water is murky, stained like tea by the tannin released through the decomposition of thousands of leaves and other organic debris. Here near Key Largo, the water is clear, flushed clean by currents, and I could easily observe a side of the forest I had never witnessed before, a universe of arching roots sunken beneath the tide. Here mangrove snapper and small fish eddied among water-logged limbs adorned with brightly colored sponges and anemones. Brown spiny seastars dotted the bottom, and algae clung to the roots in greenish, slimy mats that flowed freely with the tidal gale undercutting the island's banks. Seeing this, I felt I better understood the staggering importance of mangrove forests to both natural and human communities in tropical systems worldwide. A mangrove forest fills the sky with birds, gathers and consolidates the fabric of the land, and nourishes the sea. There is no living thing in the Keys that is not somehow influenced by mangroves.

The word *mangrove* stems from a combination of

the Portuguese word for tree (*mangue*) and the English word for a stand of trees (*grove*). They are tropical, salt-tolerant trees and shrubs that include twelve families and some fifty species. All are adapted to grow in loose, salty soil that is periodically submerged by tides. Mangroves are the dominant trees of shorelines and winding channels throughout the Keys. By trapping sediments and decayed organic material with their extensive root systems, they have helped create over two hundred islands in Florida Bay, as well as a few islands shoreward of the reef tract.

Three species of mangroves live in the Keys. The red mangrove, sometimes referred to as the "walking tree" because of the way it appears to march across the flats with its distinctive prop roots, is most prevalent along the seaward edge of the Keys' fringing mangrove forests. Its complex network of prop roots extends from the trunk, branching out and shallowly penetrating the soil below the tree. It is the pioneering tree in the mangrove forest ecosystem because of its ability to establish itself on a finger of rock or sand and then build up land around it by catching and stabilizing sediments.

The red mangrove's prop roots are produced from the lower part of the trunk, while the drop roots are generated from large branches as high as ten feet into the tree and the upper parts of the trunk. Although usually shorter, the red mangrove has been known to reach heights of nearly seventy feet. Its leaves are shiny, deep green above and paler below. Small yellow flowers appear in spring and summer, after which time the tree produces cigar-shaped propagules (seedlings) that can be as long as eleven inches before they finally drop off and float away with the tide.

Black mangroves are easily recognized by their system of shallow cable roots that radiate outward from the tree. These bristle with pneumatophores (special aerial roots that help with gaseous exchange) that extend above the mud almost eight inches, forming a carpet of spongy, fingerlike projections. The elliptical or oblong leaves, dark green on top with dense hairs on the bottom surface, are often encrusted with salt, giving the leaf an overall whitish color. The tree produces insignificant white flowers in spring and early summer, followed in late summer through early fall by small propagules, which resemble overstuffed lima beans. This species is sometimes found on the outermost edge of an island when red mangroves are absent, but in most cases it forms the middle belt of trees in the fringing mangrove forest system.

Two trees dominate the innermost band of the fringing mangrove forest. The white mangrove is usually found on dry or nearly dry areas rarely flushed by the tide. It has broad, flat, oval leaves and in the late summer and fall releases very small propagules resembling peas. Buttonwoods, although not true mangroves, are salt-tolerant trees frequently found in mangrove forests. They flower in the summer and produce a buttonlike seed case.

Mangrove reproduction

Mangroves do not produce seeds in a strict sense; instead they produce propagules, embryos that have germinated and begun development while still attached to the trees. The propagules are dropped into the water, where they continue their development, often floating far from the parent trees. The propagules can survive for a surprisingly long time in the water: White mangrove propagules last approximately thirty-five days, those of black mangroves 110 days, and propagules of red mangroves for up to a year.

When a young mangrove seedling drops from an adult, it is not quite ready to grow. It needs a period of immersion in water (red mangroves require four to five weeks) before it can resume growth. The cigar-shaped red mangrove propagule starts out floating horizontally, a strategy for getting it away from the parent tree. The pointed end begins to absorb water and grows heavy until it gradually sinks, causing the propagule

to float in an upright position. At this stage, it is ready for growth after lodging itself in a suitable substrate, such as a rocky shore or sand bar. Roots reach down into the substrate from the buried end, and within a year the distinctive prop roots will begin to develop on the young tree.

The two-to-three-inch black mangrove propagule is much smaller than that of the red mangrove, and its smaller size works to its advantage by allowing it to be carried by the tide farther up into the intertidal swamp, beyond the perimeter of red mangroves. Low tide drops it into the mud, where it splits its tough outer coating and sends out roots. This same principle works for the even smaller white mangrove seedlings, which need to work their way back beyond the red and black mangroves.

Survival mechanisms for a saltwater environment

Mangroves are the dominant trees in tropical estuarine and saltwater habitats. They are rarely found in freshwater environments. This is not because they cannot survive in fresh water (they actually will grow quite well), but because freshwater trees and shrubs outcompete them. Saltwater, fluctuating water levels, and waterlogged anaerobic sediments combine to exclude most competing trees and shrubs from mangrove swamps.

As a group, mangroves have two internal mechanisms for surviving the salty, anaerobic conditions in which they are found: They can exclude salt (not take it in) or extrude salt (take it in, transport it up the trunk, and get rid of it through glands in their leaves). Red mangroves exclude salt by separating fresh water at the root surface through a reverse osmosis process powered by high negative pressure in the xylem resulting from transpiration at the leaf surface. What little salt is assimilated is stored in the leaves and removed when leaves die and fall off the tree. The salt concentration in red mangrove sap is about one-seventieth that of seawater, but this is ten times saltier than the sap of normal freshwater plants. Black and white mangroves extrude salt through the petiole at the base of each leaf. Their sap is one-seventh as salty as seawater, but this is ten times saltier than the sap of red mangroves. Buttonwoods also exude salt through glands on the leaf

ABOVE: *High tide begins to move water through the mangroves as a storm builds over Great White Heron National Wildlife Refuge. (Photo © Jeff Ripple)* LEFT: *A great white heron is etched against a deep blue sky as it launches from its roost in the mangroves. (Photo © Bill Keogh)*

petioles.

Mangroves grow best in depositional sediment with minimal wave action. Heavy wave action prevents propagules from establishing themselves, destroys shallow root systems, and prevents the accumulation of fine anaerobic sediments. Anaerobic soil conditions are important because they limit potential competing vascular plants. Mangroves in the Keys grow on substrates that include sand, mud, rock, and peat.

Like all plants, mangroves must "breathe," and they rely on lenticels (tiny holes for gas exchange) and spongy tissue in their roots and modified branches to help them to exchange gasses. The prop roots of red mangroves possess lenticels and underground roots with open passageways (aerenchymae) for gaseous exchange. Black mangroves have up to ten thousand pneumatophores per tree to help them aerate. White mangroves have lenticels in the lower trunk for taking in oxygen for the underground aerenchymae, and sometimes peg roots and small pneumatophores as well. Although the aerial root system is ideally suited for mangrove habitat in most respects, the lenticels in the exposed part of the aerial roots are susceptible to clogging by fine suspended sediments and crude oil, attack by root borers, and prolonged flooding from artificial dikes or causeways. Any activity that covers the root systems with water or mud for extended periods will kill the trees by preventing oxygen transport to the deeper roots. Tidal fluctuation is also critical to mangroves because the tidal flow brings in clean water and nutrients; exports waste, detritus, and sulfur compounds; and disperses propagules away from the parent trees.

Mangroves can be damaged quite easily in spite of their resiliency and ability to survive in conditions unsuitable for most trees. Sudden, dramatic changes in salinity (most obviously, the increased salinity of Florida Bay); dredging, filling, and diking; human waste runoff; oil and pesticide contamination; the use of mangrove forests as dump sites; and excessive trimming by residents have all contributed to the destruction of thousands of acres of mangroves in the Keys. Hurricanes can kill mangroves through defoliation and mechanical stress, although the trees rapidly propagate in the bright sunlight.

ABOVE: *The leaves of red mangroves are a staple for Key deer. (Photo © Bill Keogh)* RIGHT: *Pencil-like pneumatophores are distinctive features of the roots of black mangroves. (Photo © Jeff Ripple)* FAR RIGHT: *A spiny lobster moves among the turtle grass bordering the outer edge of a red mangrove island. (Photo © Bill Keogh)*

Productivity of the mangrove forest

The mangrove forest is among the most productive ecosystems on Earth. In the Keys, mangroves provide food for organisms living in a complex chain of life linked with nearly every ecosystem in the Keys. I was able to witness firsthand an example of this tremendous productivity on a trip into the backcountry keys of the National Key Deer Refuge. On this particular day, Bill Keogh and I were hoping to photograph sharks moving through tidal creeks leading into a lake at the center of one of the islands. The summer sky above was a wash of blues, grays, and greens, and the dull, constant rumble of thunder reminded us that any sunlight that managed to punch through the overcast would be considered a blessing. By positioning Bill's whaler at a junction between creeks, we were able to catch lemon and nurse sharks moving past the boat from two different directions. We photographed the sharks for awhile before finally moving into the lake with the high tide. Bill poled us to the center of the lake, just in time to see a small bonnethead and a blacktip shark pass by, as well as a few mojarras and a school of twelve bonefish mudding in the coarse sediment.

As the afternoon began to wane, Bill and I headed out toward a mangrove jungle known as Crawl Key. A deep, narrow channel separated the island from an adjoining seagrass bed, allowing us to access the seagrass as well as the mangroves simply by swimming a few feet on either side of the channel. After anchoring the boat, we donned snorkeling gear and jumped overboard to drift past the mangrove roots with the incoming tide. Upon reaching the channel, I was immediately swallowed up by a vast cloud of silversides in which there was no surface or bottom or point of reference other than the thick, shimmering fog of fish that surrounded me. We drifted together for a few moments before the school flicked back upstream, leaving me breathless in an archway of brick-red roots. Brilliant orange sponges and pale anemones adorned many of the larger, deeper prop roots that remain submerged even during low tide. Hundreds of mangrove

Mangroves provide food for organisms living in a complex chain of life linked with nearly every ecosystem in the Keys

crabs clambered up the roots at my approach, sometimes dropping into the water in their frenzy to escape. Occasionally, a barracuda would slide past, its unblinking silver eye fixed in a predatory stare. The barracuda in the mangroves appeared less silver than their open-water brethren, their backs marked with olive blotches and tiger stripes on a light-green field that paled to silver along their sides and bellies. Mangrove snapper were everywhere, including a few heftier fish that nearly convinced me I should climb back into the boat for my fishing gear. It was quite simply an underwater Eden.

The basis for the tremendous productive potential of the mangrove forest is the mangrove leaf itself. A typical mangrove forest drops some three-and-a-half tons of mangrove leaves per acre per year. Because mangroves are evergreens, they shed their leaves a few at a time instead of losing all of them at once like most northern deciduous trees. This provides a steady source of nutrients throughout the year.

When a mangrove leaf dies and falls off the tree, it hits the water and begins a long process of decomposition. It takes four to five weeks in the water before the tannic acid leaches out, after which time the leaf is attacked by bacteria and protozoans that start to break it down into organic compounds, minerals, carbon dioxide, and nitrogenous waste. Amphipods and small herbivorous creatures such as crabs join the attack by helping to shred leaves into small pieces, making it easier for microbes to colonize the leaves and speed up decomposition. These bits of leaf matter and microbial hitchhikers form detritus, an essential food source for annelid worms, clams, snails, crabs, and mullet—animals at the base of the mangrove food chain. These creatures in turn are prey for mangrove snapper, tarpon, snook, bonefish, sharks, dolphins, ospreys, bald eagles, and other predators.

Although much of the litter becomes detritus, some becomes sediment and may form peat. Mangrove peat is acidic because of the organic acids released during anaerobic decomposition, and it often dissolves limestone underlying the sediment layer. The

New red mangrove seedlings become established among decaying leaves and the roots of adult mangroves. (Photo © Jeff Ripple)

characteristic rotten egg smell of mangrove swamps is from sulfuric acid released by peat and anaerobic mud that have been exposed to air at low tide.

Wildlife of the mangrove forest

You need to spend only a short amount of time exploring the shallow waters and root systems of a mangrove forest to appreciate its profusion of life. Mangroves are both home and grocery store for mammals such as the Key deer and the Key Vaca raccoon. Birds such as the great white heron, yellow-crowned night heron, great egret, green-backed heron, reddish egret,

brown pelican, double-crested cormorant, magnificent frigatebird, and white-crowned pigeon, rely on mangroves for nesting and roosting areas. Mangrove crabs forage along the roots of red mangroves, mud fiddler crabs feed among the pneumatophores of black mangroves, and mangrove periwinkles hang from roots and low branches. Mangrove water snakes and eastern diamondback rattlers sometimes prowl the roots.

North America's only crocodiles call the mangrove forests of the Keys home as well. The American crocodile is a tropical estuarine species, reaching the northern part of its range in south Florida and the Upper Keys. It is one of the most docile members of the crocodile group, preferring to make a quiet getaway rather than provoke a confrontation. Its diet consists mainly of fish, crabs, snakes, turtles, birds, and occasionally a rabbit or raccoon. During the cooler months, crocodiles can be seen basking in the sun, while during the summer they retreat to shaded areas or underground dens during the day. Because they are a tropical species, they are extremely susceptible to cold weather, so one of their most critical needs is deep

A typical mangrove island as viewed from the air. (Photo © Jeff Ripple)

water areas, where they can retreat during cold weather. Most of the crocodiles living in the Keys can be found in the Crocodile Lake National Wildlife Refuge on Key Largo. Some areas of the refuge feature deep borrow pits with ledges and islands that are ideal for crocodiles to haul themselves out on to bask. When temperatures dip too low, the crocodiles escape to the deep water of the pits.

The current crocodile population in the United States probably does not exceed six hundred animals, and no more than fifty of these are breeding adults. Approximately 65 percent of the thirty to thirty-five nests produced each year in Florida are found in the Upper Keys and northeastern Florida Bay. American crocodiles' courtship begins in early to mid-March and lasts for a period of several weeks. A male crocodile may mate with several females during this time. Eggs are laid four to six weeks after mating, usually during the last week of April or in early May.

Female crocodiles build their nests of sand, marl, or peat above the vegetation line on beaches of Florida Bay or along creek and canal banks. No vegetation is included in the nests, unlike those of the American alligator. An average clutch contains thirty-five to forty eggs, with incubation lasting eighty-five to ninety days. Female crocodiles remain near their nests during incubation, but unlike alligators, do not guard them. As with many other reptiles, proper temperature is critical to the success of a crocodile nest and in producing a fairly even ratio of male to female hatchlings. Nest temperature can depend on several factors, including the material from which the nest was made, the location of the nest, and overall weather conditions for the nesting season.

In late July to early August, crocodile eggs begin to hatch. A female will dig the babies out of the nest, take her offspring into her mouth, and carry them down to the water. However, she does not stay with them.

The young crocodiles remain together near the nest for about a month, and then disperse by early fall.

Each year, biologists conduct a census of baby crocodiles by going out at night in canoes and scooping the ten-inch babies up by hand. After weighing and measuring, each baby is permanently marked by clipping scutes (a scute is one of the series of leathery points that occurs in two rows on the animal's tail, joining at the middle of the tail) with fingernail clippers or scissors in a unique pattern that identifies where the animal came from and when it was hatched. The clipped scutes never grow back, allowing biologists to identify individual animals even when they reach adulthood.

Some baby crocodiles take up residence in large mud puddles, where they fatten up on gambusia (mosquitofish), other small fish, small snakes, and a variety of invertebrates that may share a puddle with them. If the weather during the year has been too dry, the hatchlings may not gain enough weight to make it through the winter.

Crocodiles reach sexual maturity when they are anywhere from ten to fifteen years old. By this time, they will have reached a length of at least seven feet. The largest crocodile ever recorded in Florida measured fifteen feet, six inches, but the largest animal verified in recent years was only twelve feet, four inches.

Crocodiles are faithful to a home range. If they are relocated for some reason (e.g., complaints are registered about a crocodile becoming a "nuisance" near a residential area), they have an uncanny ability to return to wherever they came from. Roads now crisscross crocodile habitat in some areas, and a few crocodiles are killed each year when they try to cross roads.

Why save mangrove forests?
Mangroves have fascinated explorers and naturalists since the arrival of the first Europeans in the 1500s. Early settlers and naturalists noted the diversity of fish, birds, and other wildlife living in mangrove wilderness. However, mangrove forests received little protection from alteration and development until the middle of the twentieth century. Since the late 1960s, heated discussions and legal battles over the importance of mangroves have erupted among planners, developers, environmentalists, and scientists attempting to decide between preservation and commercial development.

In my mind, there is nothing to debate. Mangroves are second only to tropical rain forests in productivity. Many reef fish use mangrove communities as nurseries, and almost all fish and shellfish caught by commercial and recreational fishermen spend some part of their life cycles among the submerged roots of the mangroves. These include spiny lobster, pink shrimp, snapper, tarpon, and snook. Mangroves trap and stabilize sediments in the intertidal zone, helping new islands grow and existing islands become larger. Heavy metals and nutrients that would otherwise find their way out to seagrass beds and reefs are filtered out and absorbed by filter-feeding creatures on mangrove roots. Mangrove forests also act as buffers against wave action and wind, sheltering pines, hardwoods, and even developed property from these forces during tropical storms.

Legislators seem to have paid at least lip service to the importance of mangroves by passing the Mangrove Protection Act of 1985. Under this act, it is illegal to destroy or damage mangroves in Florida (although trees are still removed by permit). In

The Keys simply cannot survive without the preservation of a substantial mangrove forest

addition, mangroves have been designated as species of special concern in the state, which affords them some additional protection.

Despite legislative protection and the obvious benefits mangroves provide, the greatest threat to mangroves in the Keys remains the impact of human development. This cannot continue. Destruction of mangrove habitat ultimately leads to a decline in commercial and sport fishing yields, both essential components of the Keys' economy. Without mangroves, the buffering qualities the forests offer against intense storm-related wave action on the islands and sedimentation on seagrass beds and offshore reefs is lost, again to the detriment of both the economy and the environment. The Keys simply cannot survive without the preservation of a substantial mangrove forest.

Sandy Beaches and Berms

*A mud fiddler crab eases out of its burrow
on a beach at Long Key State Recreation Area.*
(Photo © Jeff Ripple)

The sand fiddler eyed me warily as it eased out of its burrow, oversized right claw held high. Its jointed legs led the way, dragging it sideways out of its hole almost imperceptibly, one grain of sand at a time. Nervous and watchful, the crab rocked back and forth, its mouthparts working feverishly as it sifted through the organic debris shoved past them by its smaller, functional claw. All around me, hundreds of other sand fiddler crabs were performing the same ritual, satisfied that I posed no immediate threat as long as I was careful to stay low to the ground and move slowly. A sudden start, however, would send them scuttling back toward their burrows *en masse*. In a blink of the eye, I would be alone on the beach once again.

Beach vegetation spreading across the coastal berm at Bahia Honda State Park. (Photo © Jeff Ripple)

TOP INSET: *Hungry least tern chicks wait for their parents' return on a sandy beach in the Keys. Because sand beaches are rare in the Keys, least terns often nest on flat, gravel rooftops of homes and businesses. (Photo © by Connie Toops)* BOTTOM INSET: *Shorebirds resting as the tide goes out on a sandy beach at Bahia Honda State Park. (Photo © Jeff Ripple)*

ABOVE: *Railroad vine, beach grasses, sea grape and other coastal vegetation carpet a low dune at sunset on Bahia Honda Key, Bahia Honda State Park. (Photo © Jeff Ripple)*

The colony of sand fiddler crabs I was observing lives on a section of sandy beach along a trail running through Long Key State Recreation Area. Contrary to what many first-time visitors to the Keys might believe, most shorelines in the Keys are lined with mangroves or consist of bare bedrock; sandy beaches are few and far between. Keys with sandy beaches are located in areas where there is a break in the offshore reef or there is enough tidal current to carry large amounts of sediment to deposit on the shore.

Most shorelines in the Keys are lined with mangroves or consist of bare bedrock; sandy beaches are few and far between

Long Key at Layton and Bahia Honda, a state park about forty miles east of Key West, both have long stretches of sand beach. These beaches consist of loose carbonate sand covering bare bedrock. The sand originates from the calcareous remains of marine plants and animals that have been broken by wave action into tiny fragments. The heaviest of these fragments are filtered out by seagrass beds lying just offshore of the islands, but smaller pieces make their way in on the tides. Wrack lines of turtle grass, sargassum, and marine plant material wash up on the beach with the tide and mix with sand, helping to keep the beach from eroding away. As this organic debris decomposes, it adds critical nutrients for shore plants. Tiny amphipods (also known as hoppers) help decompose the seaweed and provide food for shorebirds, including willets, dowitchers, ruddy turnstones, semipalmated plovers, white ibis, and yellow-crowned night herons. Raccoons prowl the beaches in search of small animals, seeds, and sea turtle eggs. Other creatures roaming the sand and wrack include brown anoles and racerunners, black racers, ghost crabs and fiddler crabs, and small rats and mice.

Although by no means comparable in size to the dunes that form on Florida's east coast barrier islands, the Keys do have small dunes and coastal berms. These are created in the same manner as larger dunes. Onshore winds blow the sand inland, forming little hills of sand, shells, and organic debris from the wrack line. Beach plants such as sea oats, railroad vine, sea purslane, and puncture weed thrive in this harsh zone between the land and sea, catching and holding the sand grains with their leaves and extensive, spreading root systems. This stabilizes the dunes. Higher up near the top and behind the dunes and berms are bay bean, sand spur, bay cedar, sea lavender, saltbush, beach elder, sea oxeye daisy, and beach creeper. Stunted stands of sea grape, black bead, buttonwood, seven-year apple, and torchwood grow behind the berms.

Among the most interesting finds along the beach are seabeans, shiny seeds of different colors that wash up in the beach wrack. Legend has it that the sea heart, a floating seabean, is the heart of a drowned sailor, and that if you keep it in your pocket, you will never drown. During Prohibition, the gray nicker was a favorite seabean among rum-runners, who would gather the seeds and plant them at strategic locations where rum was brought in from the Bahamas. When the shrubs were mature, they would cut snaking paths through them. If a rum-runner was chased by a revenuer, he would throw the rum into the nickers and run along one of the trails. While trying to retrieve the rum and capture the runner, the revenuer would get tangled in the hooked spines of the thick shrubs, and the rum-runner would escape.

The Dry Tortugas
What the main tract of the Florida Keys lacks in sandy beaches is more than compensated for by the Dry Tortugas, a collection of seven islands nearly seventy miles west of Key West. They are considered a part of a larger grouping of islands known as the Sand Keys. In addition to the Dry Tortugas, the Sand Keys include the "near islands" just west of Key West and the Marquesas, a ring of seven islands approximately fifteen miles west of Key West.

Fewer than fifty species of land plants are found on the Dry Tortugas. Salty soil, drought, and frequent storms conspire to hinder plant growth. Most of the dune plants found in the Keys and elsewhere in Florida are also found here.

The beaches of the Dry Tortugas are critical nesting habitat for sea turtles and shorebirds. Hawksbill, green, leatherback, and loggerhead turtles lay their eggs

Gray nickerbean. (Photo © Jeff Ripple)

on these isolated beaches each summer. From April through September, Bush Key is alive with the flurry of wings and calls of sooty terns, noddy terns, brown pelicans, and other shorebirds. Frigatebirds nest on Long Key, while masked boobies nest on Hospital Key. Roseate terns also nest in the Dry Tortugas. The Dry Tortugas are the only significant nesting ground for sooty and noddy terns in the contiguous United States.

It is impossible to overestimate the value of beaches in the Keys and Dry Tortugas as a nesting resource for shorebirds and sea turtles. Beach development and disturbance by people, pets, and vehicles have made such habitat an increasingly rare commodity. Because isolated beaches are so hard to find, least and roseate terns frequently resort to nesting on top of the flat, gravel-topped roofs of stores throughout the Keys. Fortunately, some effort has been made to protect these birds and their nests. On Bahia Honda, the nesting areas used by least terns have been designated as sanctuaries and are permanently closed to human traffic. In the Dry Tortugas, Bush Key is closed from March through October to allow birds to nest undisturbed.

Freshwater and Transitional Wetlands

A freshwater marsh on Big Pine Key,
National Key Deer Refuge.
(Photo © Jeff Ripple)

Squish . . . my foot sank ankle deep in clear, cool water and sandy mud. *Squish* . . . my other foot followed as I stepped out into a little sawgrass marsh off one of the back trails of the National Key Deer Refuge. Dew dripped from the sawgrass and other vegetation in the marsh, and my jeans were quickly soaked to my waist. Camera in hand, I waded through the marsh, periodically stopping to photograph wildflowers while the light was gentle and the wind was calm. Dragon-flies conducted aerial sorties from the tips of sawgrass blades, pausing only to consume the mosquitoes captured on each venture. I inhaled deeply, savoring the sweet, fresh smell of the air. Freshwater marshes have always been a favorite area of mine, but this one seemed special some-

Glasswort, a common transition zone plant. (Photo © Jeff Ripple)

how. Perhaps it was because it offered such a dramatic contrast to the saltwater environments that typify the Keys. Perhaps it was because I knew how important this tiny marsh and the few other sources of fresh water on the islands are to wildlife and virtually every living thing in the Keys.

In the Keys, each puddle of rainwater is a reservoir of life—a precious gift not to be squandered. Why is fresh water so scarce? Consider that the Keys are surrounded on all sides by saltwater. The foundation of the Keys is porous limestone bedrock through which water seeps like a sieve, and much of what doesn't sink into the ground is returned to the air through evaporation, as well as through evapotranspiration by vegetation. After a rain, the shallow root systems of plants in hardwood hammocks and pinelands gather as much water as they can while it is near the surface, but the remainder runs off quickly or percolates into the bedrock. This situation is especially apparent when looking at the nature of the Key Largo limestone underlying the hardwood hammocks of the Upper Keys. This limestone is highly permeable and cracked with many fissures and cavities. Rainwater drains through the bedrock and mixes with the lower layer of salty groundwater that underlies most of the islands. Natural freshwater sites are limited to scattered, intermittently flooded basins in the hardwood hammocks and seasonally flooded depressions in the interiors of a few of the larger islands. As a result, the Upper Keys cannot support high numbers of wildlife that depend on a consistent supply of fresh water.

In the Keys, each puddle of rain water is a reservoir of life — a precious gift

The situation in the Lower Keys is somewhat different. Here, water collects at the surface much more readily and stays longer, making it more accessible to wildlife. This is because the surface limestone in many areas is cap rock, which is very dense and does not allow water to drain through quickly. Beneath the cap rock is Miami limestone—also very dense and relatively impermeable. Rainwater that percolates through the surface cap rock in uplands collects in large lenses—freshwater pools that float on top of the heavier, underlying saltwater. The size and extent of these lenses vary, depending on recent rainfall amounts, the season (wet or dry), and the size and elevation of an individual island. Generally, the major lenses of the Lower Keys are largest and the water is at its freshest during the late summer—the height of the wet season. Some lenses are smaller and saltier during the dry season.

Freshwater wetlands

The survival of Key deer and many other wildlife species in the Lower Keys depends on having reliable sources of fresh water available throughout the year. The permanent supply of fresh water is also a primary reason that pinelands are found in the Lower Keys.

When the lenses are full, they fill a variety of freshwater wetlands, including freshwater marshes, buttonwood basins, nontidal mosquito ditches, solution holes, and transitory freshwater wetlands (such as low spots in pinelands that may hold water for only a few weeks each year). These wetlands are most common in the Lower Keys (Big Pine, Little Pine, No Name, Middle and Big Torch, Little Knockemdown, Cudjoe, and Sugarloaf). The vegetation is usually dominated by sawgrass and other sedges, cattails, leather fern, grasses, and a number of herbaceous wildflowers. Small fish, crayfish, frogs, turtles, snakes, and alligators rely on these freshwater wetlands for permanent habitat, while more than seventy species of birds, including several species of wading birds and large flocks of migratory blue-winged teal and other ducks, use them as feeding areas and rest stops. Rare species of wildlife endemic to the Lower Keys that depend on freshwater wetlands include the Key striped mud turtle, Lower Keys rabbit, Key cotton rat, silver rice rat, and Key deer. A good place to see a freshwater wetland community (with alligators) is the Blue Hole Observation Platform at the National Key Deer Refuge on Big Pine Key.

OPPOSITE: *A gnarled, old buttonwood—Big Pine Key, National Key Deer Refuge. (Photo © Jeff Ripple)* OPPOSITE LEFT INSET: *Golden orb weavers are among the most common large spiders found in transition zones and hardwood hammocks throughout the Keys. (Photo © Jeff Ripple)* OPPOSITE RIGHT INSET: *A solution hole in a pine rockland on Big Pine Key. (Photo © Jeff Ripple)*

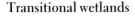

This dry, cracked mudflat illustrates the ephemeral nature of many transition zone wetlands in the Keys. (Photo © Jeff Ripple)

Transitional wetlands

Transitional wetlands, typically open salt marshes or buttonwood forests, extend from the landward edge of the fringe or scrub mangrove zone to the landward edge of the buttonwood zone, where the tropical hardwood hammocks or pinelands begin. These wetlands range from zones that are several feet wide to expanses several thousand feet across. They are usually flat and gently sloping, with a distinctive mosaic of halophytic plants growing in pockets of soil on the thin crust of caprock. These plants can survive the salty soil conditions and flooding that occurs during the spring lunar high tides.

Salt marshes in the Keys are generally desertlike flats, with only scattered groves of scrub black mangroves, red mangroves, and buttonwoods eking out an existence on the cracked mud and rock. The most observable wildlife living in these harsh conditions are a few crabs; snakes such as the black racer; and lizards, most notably green anoles, brown anoles, and six-lined racerunners. But when flooded, these marshes can be alive with small fish and feeding birds.

The austerity of the Keys' salt marshes is contrasted by the relative lushness of the buttonwood forests growing on more elevated areas landward of the salt marsh—a transition that may occur abruptly or as a smooth graduation from one zone to the next. Flat, baked mud gives way to small areas of exposed caprock outcrops peeking through meadows of Key grass, glasswort, saltwort, and saltgrass interspersed with scattered buttonwoods. False foxglove, sea oxeye daisy, and sea lavender add their splashes of color to this landscape of bright greens, reds, and white. This open fieldlike scene melds into a thicker, more wooded setting of

bromeliad-covered buttonwoods draped with Spanish moss. The fairly open canopy of the buttonwoods allows plenty of sunlight to shine through to the forest floor, encouraging the growth of grasses, sedges, cacti, and small woody plants. Seasonally flooded basins add to the diversity of this zone.

One of my favorite things to do on Big Pine Key is to take long meditative walks through buttonwood forests, especially if it's cool and cloudy. The bark of the buttonwoods on these damp days is moist and dark, with a crumbling, soil-like texture, as if the trees were trying to transport the humus at their roots upwards to the pale light streaming through the canopy. It is a marriage of earth and sky consummated through the twisted, gnarled limbs of the trees. The trees sway in the wind, the creaking of limbs sounding like the hurt, questioning cry of a child—not quite a cry of distress, but perhaps one of inner turmoil. If I sit still for awhile, sometimes Key deer will wander by, unaware of my presence. From my perch on a red mangrove root, I have watched them come to freshwater pools to drink, as shadowy and gray as the trees. I often hear them bleat, and I bleat in reply. "*Meeaah, meeahh*"—the call keeps them curious enough to stare at me inquisitively, take a few tentative steps forward, and then turn and melt back into the thickets from which they came.

When I am on a walk through the buttonwoods, I feel a presence in the forest, as if the trees and deer are watching me. There are voices all around. The squeaking of warblers, the sigh of the wind through the upper realm of the canopy, the creaking buttonwood limbs, the bleating of the deer—everything has a voice and its own language. Now I understand the communion with the forest so eloquently described by Richard Nelson in *The Island Within*: "I am never alone in this wild forest, this forest of elders, this forest of eyes."

My communion with orb weaver webs in the buttonwoods is much more tangible, especially when I spy them too late and end up draped with web on my hair and face. This, despite the conspicuous white patches of fibers the spiders have sewn into their webs to prevent such mishaps. These patches are called stabilimenta and may be laid out in vertical, circular, or crossed stripes. They are particularly ornate in the webs of silver argiopes; however, in the webs of the golden orb weavers, crablike spiny orb weavers, and arrow-shaped micrathenas, they resemble nothing more than a mish-mash of spun filament. Stabilimenta seem to serve no structural function, but they stand out clearly against the nearly invisible backdrop of the rest of the web. Biologists Thomas Eisner and Stephen Nowicki believe that stabilimenta are warning signs for birds and small mammals that may blunder into the web (same idea as a window decal on a sliding glass door). As I all too frequently prove, the warnings are not always heeded in time.

Functions and values of wetlands in the Keys

Wetlands worldwide are important for groundwater recharge, buffering the erosive effects of flood and storm waters, filtering out pollutants and sediments, and providing wildlife habitat, among other functions. In the Keys, wetlands are crucial for these same reasons. Freshwater and transitional wetlands maintain water quality by filtering stormwater runoff and absorbing nutrients from uplands. The decay of transitional wetland vegetation trickles nutrients into mangrove habitat, and when flooded during periods of extreme high tides, the mangrove habitats provide feeding and protective habitat for fish and invertebrates. Wading birds and shorebirds feed in salt marshes, salt ponds, and buttonwood wetlands during times of high water, when the usual feeding areas of these birds near shorelines and on seagrass flats in the Keys are inaccessible.

Wetlands conservation in the Keys must mean more than ensuring a consistent supply of fresh water for human consumption and adhering to government regulations and the demands of environmentalists

Although these functions are well-recognized in the Keys, wetlands are still being lost and degraded. Dredge-and-fill activities have totally or partially destroyed many freshwater wetlands, and have left others susceptible to lens drainage and saltwater intrusion. Freshwater lenses can be contaminated by inappropriately placed septic tanks, injection wells for sewage effluent, toxic discharges from commercial and industrial sites, and stormwater runoff from developed areas. Permits for filling salt marshes and buttonwood forests are still issued for the construction of residences and the installation of septic systems. Solid waste, including old appliances and even junked cars, often turns up in the dead of night. Land-clearing debris and yard waste are routinely dumped, introducing invasive exotic vegetation that crowds out native species. Given the beauty and benefits provided by wetlands, it is ludicrous to treat them with such disregard. Wetlands conservation in the Keys must mean more than ensuring a consistent supply of fresh water for human consumption and adhering to government regulations and the demands of environmentalists. Wetlands must be restored or set aside for preservation wherever possible because they are more than a resource; they are a precious strand in the web of human, plant, and wildlife communities that make the Keys "Paradise."

OPPOSITE TOP: *Limestone bedrock shows through the sparse vegetation of the transition zone at The Nature Conservancy's Torchwood Hammock Preserve. (Photo © Jeff Ripple)* OPPOSITE LEFT INSET: *Seaside gentian, a beautiful wildflower of the transition zone. (Photo © Jeff Ripple)* OPPOSITE RIGHT INSET: *The brown anole, a native of islands throughout the Caribbean, was accidentally introduced to the Florida Keys and has spread rapidly throughout much of Florida. (Photo © Jeff Ripple)*

Pinelands

A red-shouldered hawk, National Key Deer Refuge.
(Photo © Jeff Ripple)

At the edge of day, just after sunrise and for about a half-hour before nightfall, the rocky pine forests of the Lower Keys glow with a soft, warm light. The shadows cast by the sun's low angle sharpen the varied textures of this landscape of wood and stone: the rough bark of the pines; the pale jagged chunks of limestone littered about the forest floor; the swordlike fronds of the silver palms and saw palmettos. It is a magical, delicate light that brushes the Key deer with gold when they materialize from the pines to feed and play. The light illuminates the fleecy, translucent tips of the sparse grasses swaying in the breeze, and splashes pink upon the breast of a red-shouldered hawk staring down from its perch on a pine limb, its sharp eyes scanning the ground for the false

The aftermath of a prescribed burn on a pine rockland on Big Pine Key. (Photo © Jeff Ripple)

move of an anole or a snake. Overhead, a pair of bald eagles soar, their chocolate and white bodies etched against the clear blue sky before they finally tilt toward Earth and drop low to disappear beneath the horizon of pine tops. This is the time when the pinelands seem most alive, and it is the time that I love best to walk through these woods and photograph.

Rocky pinelands are not widespread in the Keys. Unlike the mangrove forests and tropical hardwood hammocks, their domain is limited to the Lower Keys, primarily Big Pine Key, Little Pine Key, No Name Key, Summerland Key, Cudjoe Key, and a few other small islands in the Florida Bay backcountry. There are several reasons for this confined geographic coverage, but the lack of a permanent freshwater supply on most keys has historically been the major limiting factor.

Currently, the slow rise of sea level is believed to be the most significant natural force determining the extent and health of pinelands in the Lower Keys. The pinelands are not being flooded out, but because slash pines are not salt-tolerant, increased levels of salt in groundwater and in the soil are killing many trees. In a typical sea-level rise scenario, pines in fringing, low-lying areas closest to the shoreline are the first to die out when salt invades the groundwater and soil. They are usually replaced by species such as mangroves and buttonwoods, which thrive in saltier conditions. As time goes on and sea level continues to rise, groundwater and soil become progressively more saline over a broader area, and even pines toward the center of the community begin to fail. Eventually the pineland community is reduced to pine snags and a relict mixture of pineland plants and other plants better able to survive the saltier conditions.

This process was dramatically played out in the death of the only known pine forest in the Upper Keys. Living pines were found on upper Key Largo through the late 1800s. By the early 1930s, however, only a few old trees remained, and by the 1950s, no live pines were left. Today only stumps and a scattering of plant species common to pinelands remain as testimony to Key Largo's pine forest. In the Lower Keys, biologists have documented a decline of pines due to rising sea level over the last seventy years, and the trend is expected to continue. While the decline is fairly slow at this point, unchecked human consumption of water drawn from freshwater lenses will quicken the process, with devastating results for the pineland ecosystem. Permanent saltwater canals have also been shown to substantially reduce the depth and extent of adjacent freshwater lenses. This emphasizes the need to protect existing pinelands from human development and limit the amount of fresh water drawn from the lenses.

Pineland ecology

Pine forests in the Lower Keys grow in thin, nutrient-poor soil that covers rocky outcrops of Miami oolitic limestone. Pocked with solution holes and littered with chunks of limestone, it seems improbable that anything of substance could grow here at all. But the pinelands are a repository of wondrous living things—plants, birds, mammals, and insects. Furthermore, different areas of pineland can vary markedly from site to site. Some may have a low shrub layer and a profusion of silver palms and thatch palms, beneath which the understory consists of scattered grasses poking up through the smooth, bare limestone. In other areas, the hardwood subcanopy is dense and tall.

The pinelands are a repository of wondrous living things — plants, birds, mammals, and insects

Like many forest systems, pinelands are composed of an upper canopy, an understory or subcanopy, and a sparse layer of groundcover plants. The upper canopy is dominated by south Florida slash pine, a variety of slash pine found only in southern Florida. The south Florida variety differs from the slash pine common throughout the southeastern coastal plain from South Carolina to Louisiana in several respects. One such difference is the manner in which it produces thicker-stemmed seedlings that undergo what is known as a "grass" stage. During the grass stage, the seedlings develop a dense growth of long needles and remain in the ground layer. The thick growth of needles protects the growing tip of a seedling against the ground fires that periodically sweep through a pineland. If a fire occurs at this stage, only the leaves

Bahama cassia—common pineland wildflower and larval food for various sulphur butterflies in the Keys. (Photo © Jeff Ripple)

The Florida leafwing, a butterfly endemic to South Florida and the Keys. The markings on the undersides of the wings resemble a dead leaf to camouflage the butterfly when it is resting. (Photo © Jeff Ripple)

TOP INSET: *Sunset over pinelands, National Key Deer Refuge. (Photo © Bill Keogh)* BOT-
TOM INSET: *A South Florida slash pine seedling at grass stage, Big Pine Key. (Photo © Jeff
Ripple)*

87

are singed and the thick trunk is saved. The grass stage may last five or more years before the tree finally continues its development into a sapling. Adult pines are protected by a thick bark that does not easily burn. Another fire adaptation is the way in which most of the needles are found at the crown of the tree. Lower limbs fall off the tree as it grows taller, until the lowest limbs may be thirty feet high. Cool surface fires are necessary at this stage to keep understory plants far below the level of the crowns of the pines. Otherwise, flames could shoot up into the tops of the trees, killing them.

A distinctive feature of Keys pine rocklands is the large number of palms found in the understory, the most prominent of which are the silver palm and the brittle thatch palm. Both of these palms are rare outside the Keys and extreme southern Florida and are protected from collection. There is a heavy West Indian influence in the species of plants found in the understory as well, with poisonwood, black bead, myrsine, locustberry, pisonia, and golden creeper being among the most common. The seeds of West In-

dian plants were originally deposited by birds or arrived on ocean currents or winds from tropical storms. They prosper because of the abundant rainfall and infrequency of freezing temperatures.

Grasses, ferns, and beautiful wildflowers comprise most of the pineland ground layer. Common grasses include bluestem, dropseed, and three-awn. Ferns are especially common around sinkholes and include ladder brake and pine fern. Wildflowers, such as purple blazing star, yellow-top, yellow colic-root, snowberry, rosy fleabane, tickseed, and yellow star grass, are among the species that brighten the ground layer throughout

Bahama morning glory. (Photo © Jeff Ripple)

Florida box turtles are most often seen in the early morning or late afternoon hours as they move through the low brush of the pinelands. (Photo © Jeff Ripple)

the year. Rare plants include Big Pine partridge pea, brown-haired snout bean, and noseburn.

The role of fire in Keys pinelands

Fire is essential to maintaining the integrity of Keys pinelands. Although fires historically occurred during the late spring or early summer as a result of lightning strikes, most fires now are intentionally set as part of prescribed management plans for pineland habitat. Fire prunes back the hardwood understory that would eventually shade out pine seedlings and replace the pines. Surface fires also prevent a buildup of dead wood and dried organic matter that could lead to uncontrolled wild fires capable of reaching into the canopy of the pines and destroying mature trees.

In the aftermath of a typical prescribed fire, some of the lower branches and needles of a few mature pines are scorched, but only a few trees are actually killed by the flames. In the understory, the aboveground portion of hardwood shrubs is usually destroyed, but these plants will resprout from underground root systems within a few months. The intensity of the fire is also erratic, with unburned patches remaining within large blackened areas. The unburned patches are important for providing food and shelter for pineland creatures, as well as acting as a seed source for replenishing the pine community's plant life. While the ecology of Keys pinelands and many of the techniques for managing them with fire are similar to pine forests in the Everglades and Big Cypress Swamp, there are many differences, and the complete role of fire in the Keys and the frequency with which fires should occur are only now receiving scientific attention.

The diminutive Key deer

The rocky pinelands of National Key Deer Refuge on

Big Pine Key is perhaps the most accessible place to see many of the wildlife species native to the Florida Keys. This habitat is the stronghold of the refuge's namesake—the Key deer—which evolved from white-tailed deer living on the Florida mainland. Thousands of years ago, sea level rose, isolating the deer on what is now the Lower Florida Keys. Although Key deer range from Johnson Key west to Sugarloaf Key, the primary deer population is concentrated on Big Pine Key.

Key deer are toylike compared to other subspecies of Virginia whitetails, including the relatively small deer living on the mainland in south Florida. Adult males weigh approximately eighty pounds, while females average sixty-four pounds. At birth, a Key deer fawn weighs less than four pounds. Coats range in color from reddish brown to gray (especially in older deer). The black facial mask is especially noticeable in males.

Key deer bucks, like other whitetails, grow a new set of antlers each year. As a buck ages, his antlers become larger and more developed. A Key deer buck's antlers develop spikes at two years, forks at three years, six points by four years, and eight points by five years. Males rarely begin breeding before their third year, when a full rack has developed.

Most deer live to be eight or nine years old. Does generally do not breed before their second or third year. Breeding begins in September, with activity peaking in October and November. Most fawns are born in April and May after a 204-day gestation period. More than 20 percent of the fawns die within the first six months. Dogs and drownings in mosquito ditches when fawns are only a few days old are among the most common causes of fawn mortality. More Key deer die by being hit by cars than from any other cause—an average of forty-two each year.

Key deer for the most part are solitary animals, although they frequently gather in small mixed groups. Bucks sometimes form small herds during the nonbreeding season. Small bands of deer gather in open areas from dawn to dusk to feed and escape insects, especially during the summer and early fall. Daylight hours are spent under cover in hardwood hammocks and buttonwood forests.

Key deer seem to prefer the diversity of food and shelter provided by pinelands and hardwood hammocks. During the heat of the day, I find them resting in the deep shadows of hardwood hammocks or in the shade beneath saw palmettos or silver palms. In the evening, I watch them move into open grassy areas and buttonwoods, as well as into the mangrove fringe near the water's edge. They feed on more than 160 kinds of plants, but their staples include the leaves of red mangrove; the fruits of black mangrove, silver palm and brittle thatch palm; Indian mulberry; blackbead; wild dilly; acacia; pencil flower; and various grasses. Prescribed burning in pinelands benefits the deer because it stimulates new growth from the newly cleared ground and from existing root stocks of mature plants (such as saw palmetto, palms, and hardwoods) that were burned. A year-round supply of fresh water is essential to the survival of the deer, emphasizing the importance of freshwater wetlands and solution holes and the conservation of underlying freshwater lenses. These animals are good swimmers and are sometimes seen swimming between islands, especially during times of drought, when they move from outlying islands to Big Pine and No-Name keys.

Key deer seem to prefer the diversity of food and shelter provided by pinelands and hardwood hammocks

Key deer were nearly hunted and harassed to extinction in the early part of this century. Conservationist and cartoonist J. "Ding" Darling exposed the plight of the deer with his cartoons in 1934, depicting hapless tiny deer being slaughtered by hulking hunters and slathering dogs. By 1939, public pressure forced the Florida Legislature to ban the hunting of Key deer. However, population levels still remained low as a result of continued habitat destruction (in the late 1940s, the herd was estimated at between twenty-five and eighty animals). Several private organizations and the U.S. Fish and Wildlife Service recognized the need to preserve deer habitat and established the National Key Deer Refuge in 1957 in an effort to set aside land needed to protect the herd. In a further attempt to protect the species, the Key deer was listed as endangered in 1967. Jack Watson, the first warden of the National Key Deer Refuge, is credited with almost single-handedly bringing the deer population up from its mid-century low to a herd that exceeded 350 animals in the 1970s. The population now has stabilized at around three hundred deer.

Although feeding Key deer was once common practice, it is now prohibited by federal law because of the negative consequences the feeding has on the deer. Deer accustomed to being hand-fed lose their natural wariness of humans and become what many longtime Keys residents call "zombie" deer—deer that are easy targets for poachers and too often are the victims of car-deer collisions as they panhandle by the roadside. Feeding deer the wrong foods (such as the loaves of white bread I have seen stacked up on the side of the road, with deer clustered around) can also harm their health by encouraging them to seek out human "junk" food rather than relying on their own natural diet. Finally, when many deer concentrate around human feeding areas, they become more susceptible to contagious disease, fighting, or other density-related mortalities. They may drown in canals, be attacked by dogs, or be harassed by people.

Other pineland wildlife

In contrast to the heavy West Indian influence on the composition of pineland vegetation, wildlife in Keys pinelands originates almost entirely from southeastern, temperate North America. There is also a noticeable lack of species diversity in the wildlife found here. Ecologists consider this a result of the "peninsula effect." Much historical and ecological debate has raged over why this occurs. Most researchers agree that the isolation and relatively limited extent of pineland habitat in the Lower Keys has had an important role in limiting the original access of pineland denizens and their subsequent recolonization after catastrophic events, such as hunting or hurricanes. In the case of breeding land birds in the Lower Keys, the peninsula

Some of the birds that might be encountered during a morning or early evening stroll through the pinelands include the northern cardinal, red-shouldered hawk, gray kingbird, palm warbler, white-crowned pigeon, and Antillean nighthawk

effect is especially noticeable. Some seventy species inhabit northern Florida, while only forty are found in the southern peninsula region. In the Keys, only twenty land species breed, and this number includes a few West Indian birds. Migratory birds, however, use the pinelands heavily for feeding and resting.

Ribbon snakes, black racers, eastern diamondback rattlesnakes, red rat snakes, Florida box turtles, and brown anoles are among the other more conspicuous animals found in Key pinelands. Some of the birds that might be encountered during a morning or early evening stroll through the pinelands include the northern cardinal, red-shouldered hawk, gray kingbird, palm warbler, white-crowned pigeon, and Antillean nighthawk. During the fall and spring migrations, thousands of migratory warblers and other songbirds, as well as many raptors, may appear in pineland areas.

The future of the pinelands

Nightfall comes quickly to the pinelands. Once the sun sinks below the treetops, the soft, golden light fades and the shadows gradually creep from the forest floor up the trunks of the pines until they reach the sky. After a hike to photograph the sunset, Bill Keogh and I paused near the trailhead to Watson's Hammock one autumn evening to watch the full moon rise. The moon floated just above the pines, a luminous golden globe bathed in the afterglow of the sunset. As it rose higher above the trees, it diminished in size, yet increased in intensity, casting its pale light across the landscape. Thousands of fireflies rose from the grasses, their spasms of fire and the moon's cool glow creating a fascinating juxtaposition of light. We wondered how and why the fireflies were able to synchronize their flashings so that a single group illuminated an entire area with their glow. What was the significance of the number of times each firefly flashed and the intervals between flashes? Why did each firefly seem to maintain a constant glow when it rested on the tip of a blade

Key deer groom in a thicket on Big Pine Key, National Key Deer Refuge. (Photo © Jeff Ripple)

of grass or leaf?

Other elusive considerations entered our discussion that evening as well, some of which centered on the future of pinelands. Rocky pineland areas are among the most desirable construction sites in the Lower Keys. The land is under constant siege by developers and residents wanting to expand their communities and businesses to accommodate the influx of tourists and new residents to the area. However, conservationists worry that too much land has already been developed and warn that the islands will not be able to withstand additional development. As an example, tension on Big Pine Key runs high between federal agencies responsible for environmental protection and residents pressing for continued growth. At the center of the debate is the Key deer and its habitat requirements. While the deer is the focal point of the debate, it is the entire pineland community that is at stake. Fresh water and dry land are in limited supply, and both humans and wildlife are competing for the same resources. However, people do not come first, nor do the Key deer. Lower Keys residents should not fear being thrown off the islands any more than they should expect development to be allowed to continue at the expense of deer and other wild creatures.

The pinelands are neither renewable nor expendable. A delicate balance must be maintained between nature and humans. Once everyone living on or visiting the Keys recognizes this fundamental precept, we will advance one critical step closer to preserving the pinelands and other ecosystems of the Keys.

Hardwood Hammocks

The Key Largo woodrat is an endangered species restricted to tropical hardwood hammocks on Key Largo.
(Photo © by Barry Mansell)

The morning light was still gentle as I plunged through the thick tangle of vines and shrubs bordering a tract of tropical hardwood hammock on North Key Largo. I was searching for an elusive little creature known as the Key Largo woodrat, an endangered rodent found only in hammocks on Key Largo. Because of the woodrat's rarity and retiring nature, I didn't expect to find the animal itself, but I did hope to come across its wigwam-style stick nest.

Luck was with me. I had traveled no more than fifty yards into the hammock when I stumbled upon a woodrat nest snuggled into the leaf litter at the base of a pigeon plum tree. The nest was an almost perfect textbook example of woodrat workmanship. Measuring about five feet long

Limber caper—a native to South Florida and the Keys. It is also known as the "false tooth plant." (Photo © Jeff Ripple)

and three to four feet wide, it had two exit openings and a more spacious entrance. Root fibers, bark, twigs, leaves, bits of limestone, and snail shells were used for construction material. Dropping to my hands and knees, I peered into the opening. No woodrat peered back. The main passageway, carefully lined with leaves and chewed root fibers, led down into the nest and seemed in good repair. More than likely, the woodrat was either asleep inside or watching me from the safety of a tree, chewing nervously and wishing I would leave.

The Key Largo woodrat looks more like one of those cutesy watercolor rodents rendered on the front of an English greeting card than does its exotic cousin, the European rat. The woodrat's eyes and ears are large and round, and its soft, dense brown and white fur is mixed with reddish and cream tones. The woodrat grows to about sixteen inches long—half of that length being a tail covered by very fine hairs (unlike the scaled tails of European rats). Woodrats are excellent climbers, a skill they put to good use as they gather the fruit, buds, leaves, and seeds of native hardwoods that form the bulk of their diet. They are also known as "pack rats" or "trade rats" because of their affinity for collecting snail shells, animal skulls, rings, or anything bright and shiny. As with the snail shells and bits of limestone scattered about the nest in front of me, these items often find themselves incorporated as ornamentation or building material in a woodrat nest.

Tropical hardwood hammocks are considered to be the keystone habitat for life on land in the Keys, much like the reefs are to the region's marine areas

Every woodrat nest I have encountered has been constructed at the base of a large hardwood, most noticeably pigeon plum, but woodrats have been known to build high in the branches, safe from ground predators. Although stick nests seem to be the dwellings of choice, woodrats will also live in limestone crevices and holes in the stumps of trees.

An abandoned woodrat nest is not necessarily a vacant one; snakes find empty woodrat nests quite cozy. Red and yellow rat snakes, eastern diamondback rattlesnake, Key Largo coral snake (unique because this Keys subspecies lacks distinct yellow bands bordering its red and black bands), and the rare rimrock crowned snake are among the species that may move in after the original occupant has moved out.

Unfortunately, Key Largo woodrats have suffered a dramatic decline due to human disturbance and the loss of mature hardwood hammock habitat. Due to predation by cats and dogs and competition from European rats, they do not fare well near residential areas. It is estimated that less than two thousand acres of suitable habitat for the woodrat remains. This sobering statistic stuck with me as I left the nest and continued on my hike through the hammock.

Key Largo woodrats are not the only wildlife that rely heavily on tropical hardwood hammocks. For neotropical migratory birds, these hammocks offer a critical sanctuary in which to rest and forage before continuing on their journey. Tropical hardwood hammocks are considered to be the keystone habitat for life on land in the Keys, much like the reefs are to the region's marine areas. Lush and green, brimming with a host of rare creatures, they represent the pinnacle of forest development in southern Florida. Found only at the extreme southern tip of Florida and in the Keys, they are regarded as one of North America's rarest ecosystems. Figures from 1976 indicate that only 7 percent of the original upland habitats remained, and the percentage drops with each passing year as development takes its toll. Fortunately, nearly all of Upper Key Largo is still hardwood hammock, protected from development by the Key Largo Hammock State Botanical Site and the Crocodile Lake National Wildlife Refuge. Lignumvitae Key State Botanical Site in the Middle Keys and some of the islands in the national wildlife refuges in the Lower Keys also have significant areas of hammock remaining. A patchwork of hammock remnants exists throughout the Middle and Lower Keys, including the Florida Keys Land and Sea Trust's Crane Point Hammock on Key Vaca (Marathon) and The Nature Conservancy's Torchwood Hammock on Little Torch Key.

Most plants in tropical hardwood hammocks in the Keys originated from the West Indies, arriving as seeds passed from the crops of migrating birds or borne upon the winds of tropical storms. More than two hun-

ABOVE: *Poisonwood leaves. The yellow margins of the leaves and black resinous stains on the bark are distinguishing characteristics of this beautiful but poisonous tree. (Photo © Jeff Ripple)* LEFT: *Poisonwood fruit after a heavy rain. Poisonwood fruit is a critical food for threatened white-crowned pigeons. (Photo © Jeff Ripple)*

Beautyberry, a shrub found near the edges of tropical hardwood hammocks in the Keys. It is an important food plant for butterflies and wildlife. (Photo © Jeff Ripple)

dred species of trees, shrubs, and plants live in Keys hammocks; thirty-six of these are currently listed as endangered or threatened. On the 2,700-acre Key Largo Hammock State Botanical Site, eighty-four species of plants and animals are designated protected species.

Like many other forest communities, a tropical hardwood hammock can be structurally divided by plant species into a canopy or overstory, midstory, understory, and groundcover. The canopy is composed of the largest trees, which in the Keys includes wild tamarind, gumbo-limbo, Jamaica dogwood, willow bustic, paradise tree, and poisonwood. Young trees of canopy species, in addition to smaller mature trees such as pigeon plum, black ironwood, cinnamon bark, Spanish stopper, milkbark, and blackbead, complete the midstory. Beneath the midstory, tropical shrubs dominate the diverse aggregation of understory plants, including white indigoberry, false boxwood, and two

species of wild coffee. Woody shrubs and vines such as chewstick, snowberry, cheeseweed, hog plum, cockspur, and limber caper compete with saplings of midstory and overstory species for the limited light and nutrients found at this level. Groundcover is usually sparse due to the faint light reaching the forest floor through the thick overstory. It generally consists of seedlings of overstory species and sometimes wild bamboo, a native grass.

At the edges of the hammock, the vegetation becomes brushy and thick with sun-loving Bahama strongbark, lancewood, soldierwood, wild sage, sweet acacia, scarlet bush, geiger, seven-year apple, saffron plum, and wild cotton. Many of these plants have colorful or fragrant flowers that attract flying insects. This surrounding dense growth forms a barrier that helps shelter the inner sanctum of the hammock from wind, salt spray, and other elements that would dry out or damage hammock trees and soil.

A Liguus tree snail, Crocodile Lake National Wildlife Refuge. (Photo © Jeff Ripple)

The hammock relies on other mechanisms to retain moisture and nutrients as well. Its dense overstory provides shade from the hot sun, moderating temperatures within the hammock and protecting the rich soil from moisture loss. The spongy layer of decaying leaves and twigs that carpets the forest floor supplies nutrients essential to hammock plants and serves as a critical seed repository that enables a hammock to replenish itself as older trees die. This humus layer also acts as a giant sponge, absorbing rain and keeping the water near the surface for use by hammock vegetation and wildlife before it can percolate into the limestone bedrock. This function is especially important during the winter dry months, when little rain falls and water is more precious than ever.

Most flowering and fruit production in tropical hardwood species occurs during the Key's May-through-October rainy season, although late winter and early spring rains stimulate flower growth and new leaf production in species such as wild tamarind, gumbo-limbo, and mahogany. New growth in tropical plants is frequently bright red, making the hammocks a colorful place in which to hike, especially after a rain. The bark of many trees also contributes splashes of color to the uniform green of tropical foliage. Pigeon plum and poisonwood have multicolored trunks of orange, gray, and brown. The shaggy, peeling bark of gumbo-limbo ranges in color from a deep red to an iron gray. Milkbark or "cheap birch" is white and looks much like the northern birch, although the two are not related. On the trees on Lignumvitae Key, lichens stain the bark of many tree species a rich yellow.

The history behind the names of many tropical hardwood plants is as fascinating as the plants themselves. Take the milkbark for instance. Its nickname "cheap birch" stems from its uncanny resemblance to northern birch, a fact that has not gone unnoticed by migratory yellow-bellied sapsuckers. They hammer feverishly at the bark of these trees, expecting to draw the sap and insects they are accustomed to getting from northern birch. No amount of effort on the sapsuckers' part will get the trees to produce, and the birds fly off disappointed—hence the nickname "cheap birch."

The history behind the names of many tropical hardwood plants is as fascinating as the plants themselves

Gumbo-limbo, on the other hand, is a prolific producer of sap. The word *gumbo* refers to anything of slave origin, and *limbo* ("bird lime") is derived from the use of the tree's sticky sap by slaves to catch birds. Because slaves were not allowed to use weapons, they improvised, and bird lime became a valuable hunting tool. To catch a bird, all a slave had to do was strip bark off a favored perching branch so that when a bird landed, it would get stuck in the oozing sap. The bird was then eaten or sold as a caged pet. Gumbo-limbo is also known as the "tourist tree" (because its red, peeling bark resembles sunburned skin), *El Indio des Nudo* (in Mexico and Central America, literally "the naked Indian"), and gum elemi (a name probably stemming from its many former medicinal uses in poultices, salves, and teas). This tree is popular in the Caribbean because if a branch is broken off and planted in the ground, it will grow. On my hikes through hammocks in Everglades National Park and on Upper Key Largo, I've noticed that gumbo-limbo branches strewn about the forest floor as a result of Hurricane Andrew have resprouted, ensuring the continued presence of these trees in the hammocks.

Jamaica dogwood is a common native deciduous tree that in the spring loses its leaves and produces small, pink, popcorn-shaped flowers. It gets its name not because of any relation to the familiar dogwood trees of temperate regions, but because its wood was used in shipbuilding to fashion a small wedge called a "dog." The dog's purpose was to hold planking to the keel of a boat; Jamaica dogwood was favored because the tree produces a chemical similar to rotenone (an invertebrate poison), making it highly resistant to marine wood borers and general decay. If you hike through a hammock in the Keys and find a dead piece of wood on the forest floor, it's probably Jamaica dogwood; a fallen gumbo-limbo branch that doesn't sprout will rot in six months. The rate of decay varies among tree species, based on the chemical composition of the wood. Jamaica dogwood is also called the "fish poison tree" or the "fish fuddle tree" because the dried roots and buds were once used by fishermen to paralyze the gills of fish, making them easy to scoop off the

ABOVE: *Lignum vitae seed. (Photo © Jeff Ripple)* LEFT: *Palms growing in the understory of the Florida Land and Sea Trust's Crane Point Hammock on Key Vaca at Marathon. (Photo © Jeff Ripple)*

water's surface.

Pigeon plum and poisonwood are two trees frequently confused for one another because of the orange spotting on their otherwise gray trunks. Pigeon plum belongs to the same family as seagrape and can be identified by the way its leaf stem actually wraps itself around the twig like a bracelet. Its Latin name (*Cocoloba diversifolia*) refers to the various sizes of the leaves, which on a mature tree can be fairly small or as big as your face. Pigeon plum is a dioecious tree, meaning there are two sexes. Sexing the tree is easier than you might expect. A nearly foolproof method is to examine the trunk for scratch marks. Raccoons spare no effort to climb these trees for the fruit, which is found only on females. If there are no scratch marks up the trunk of the tree, you can bet it's a male.

Poisonwood truly lives up to its name. Belonging to the same family as mangos, pistachios, and cashews, it is most easily distinguished from the pigeon plum by the black sticky patches on the leaves and bark, no matter how small the tree. These oily-looking black spots are actually pools of resin that have oxidized after being exposed to the air. The resin contains a poisonous oil called urushiol, which causes an allergic dermatological reaction if you happen to get it on your skin. You won't react initially, but soon severe rashes and blistering will occur on the affected area. Because poisonwood is so common in Keys' hammocks, you should always wear long pants and long sleeves during a hike, and take care not to lean against the trees or grab their branches. Do not eat the fruit. Despite the trees' poisonous effect on human visitors, poisonwood fruit is among the most valuable food sources to fruit- and seed-eating birds in the Keys.

Lignum vitae is a slow-growing, early successional stage tree that prefers higher spots in the hammock. In the spring and early summer, it produces delicate, pale blue flowers. Lignum vitae literally means "wood of life," and old medical books recommended the use of its resin (known as guaiac gum) for the treatment of gout, tonsillitis, neuralgia, and syphilis. At one time, the hard, heavy wood was common material for propeller shaft bearings in steamships, pulley sheaves, and deadeyes, and as a replacement for metal in bearings.

A green anole, one of the Keys' native lizards. (Photo © Jeff Ripple)

Gumbo limbo, a beautiful native tree of tropical hardwood hammocks. (Photo © Jeff Ripple)

Although it is common throughout the Upper and Middle Keys, lignum vitae's stronghold is in the hammock on its namesake island, Lignumvitae Key. Current estimates place some 1,500 trees on the island, but this number is decreasing because as the hammock matures, the lignum vitaes are being shaded out by larger overstory trees. A scale problem and the lingering effects of a recent drought are also contributing to the gradual decline of lignum vitaes on the key.

Mahogany is another common deciduous tropical tree and one of the few tropical trees to produce a single annual ring. Most trees in the Keys produce several rings a year, the number depending on the amount of rainfall received. A wide band of rings is produced during a rainy period and a narrow band of rings during a dry period. In the Caribbean, there are usually two rainy periods (early summer and late summer) and sometimes three if a significant amount of rain falls during the winter.

Mahogany is most easily identified by its distinctive seed pods, which appear in late spring and throughout the summer. When pressed to describe these unusual pods, I fall back on the description offered by Jeanne Parks, a good-natured, seasoned biologist who probably knows more about hardwood hammocks than anyone else in the Keys. According to Jeanne, they resemble nothing less than "green goose eggs sitting on golf tees." When a pod is ripe, it turns brittle and splits open, exposing the seeds, which are thin, papery samara similar to maple seeds. Mahogany is also a copious producer of tannin, a natural insect repellent and a very bitter-tasting one at that. In the tropics, the more tannin a tropical tree produces, the better its chances are of resisting attacks by insects.

Mahogany was commercially harvested for furniture and other wood products off North Key Largo until the late 1960s. The old mahoganies of the Keys grew to a tremendous size, and you can still find stumps measuring six feet across. Pilots flying over Key Largo during World War II described the hammocks of North Key Largo as looking like they had mushrooms growing from the canopy. The "mushrooms" were in fact the crowns of mahoganies towering over the rest of the canopy, spreading to the mushroom shape. Unfortunately, most of the old trees are gone, and it will be decades before the new generation reaches the immense proportions of their parents.

Solution holes and wildlife

I walked further into the interior of the hammock until the sounds of the road faded and I could hear nothing except the wind stirring the top of the canopy. There was hardly any groundcover, and walking was easy on the springy mat of dead leaves and fibrous soil that covered the forest floor. Occasionally, an outcrop of limestone would break through this organic carpet, or a tree tipped up during a storm would leave a shallow pit, exposing a multitude of creeping and scuttling creatures for which crumbling rock, soil, and decaying leaves combined to create a universe unto itself.

Pressing on through a grove of young trees where the undergrowth was somewhat thicker and walking was considerably more difficult, I finally stopped at the edge of a large solution hole. Solution holes, if they are deep enough, actually reach the water table and were the original wells of the Florida Keys. Settlers expanded many solution holes, creating wells to collect rain water. These were later followed by cisterns, which were always stocked with gambusia (mosquitofish) to eat the mosquito larvae that invariably hatched and grew to adulthood in the quiet water.

Solution holes are important to the hammock ecosystem because they provide fresh water for trees and wildlife. They also are the only areas in the hammocks that have significant accumulations of soil, sometimes as much as twelve inches at the bottom. During the

winter season, pioneering farmers cleared surrounding vegetation and planted crops in the holes. The crops, usually coconuts, pineapples, and peppers, were then shipped out on small boats to meet with larger ships in the Gulf Stream, and from there were transported to New York for sale at the winter market.

Solution holes vary dramatically in width and depth, ranging from the size of a dinner plate with no apparent bottom to a broad, shallow depression. The solution hole before me was about twenty-five feet across and maybe ten feet deep. Now, in the middle of April, it was dry, and I carefully made my way down its slope to the bottom and found a comfortable seat in the leaves. Leaning back against a slab of fossilized brain coral, I stared out from my limestone bowl and let the atmosphere of the hammock permeate my senses. A brown anole basked nearby in a patch of open sunlight, constantly adjusting itself on its branch to maintain just the right angle for maximum warming. The sun was higher and hotter now, and light flickered through the canopy in blinding kaleidoscopic patterns that danced with the breeze across the deep shadow of surrounding foliage and forest floor. I breathed in deeply, savoring the hammock's sweet, musky incense.

It's amazing how much you notice if you stay rooted to a single spot and open your mind and senses to what surrounds you. By focusing on the fossilized coral embedded in the limestone walls of the solution hole, I slowly became aware of its texture and patterns, the growth of moss and the accumulation of leaf litter along its ribbed contours, and the peculiar greenish glow it reflected as light filtered down from the canopy. Revealed within the walls of this hole, within this stone, was the history of the hammock and indeed, the history of the Upper Keys themselves. Generations of coral had settled layer upon layer to form the foundation of life for first a thriving reef and now, thousands of years later, the shallow, fibrous soil and thrust of trees reaching toward the sky.

I was jarred from my meditation of reef and roots by a hurried flapping overhead. Three white-crowned pigeons shot out through an opening in the canopy and then were gone. These birds are incredibly shy and fast and rarely allow you the opportunity to focus on them, much less attempt a close approach. I sometimes see them flying solo or in groups of two or three as they pass quickly over mangrove islands in the Lower Keys backcountry.

Butterflies are integral parts of the hammock ecosystem because of their role as pollinators

White-crowned pigeons are found at the southern tip of Florida in Everglades National Park, the Florida Keys, and throughout the Caribbean. Slate-gray with a distinctive white forehead patch, they are about the size of common park pigeons (rock doves). White-crowned pigeons are listed as threatened throughout most of their range and, although protected in the United States, they are still hunted for food on many islands in the Caribbean. This may in part explain their extreme shyness.

Biologists estimate the current breeding population of white-crowns in Florida at about five thousand pairs. The pigeons are most abundant in the Keys during the May-through-September breeding season. They nest on isolated mangrove islands, free from raccoons and human activity, from Key Biscayne through the Marquesas Keys. Most of these islands are within the boundaries of Everglades National Park in the Upper Keys and the wildlife refuges in the Lower Keys.

There are two nesting periods—one lasting from May through June and the other from July into September. The second breeding period coincides with the ripening of poisonwood fruit, an important food source, and it is during this period that most young pigeons are hatched. Although white-crowns feed on the fruit of some thirty-five species of trees, poisonwood, blolly, and strangler and short-leaf figs are their favorites. Of these trees, poisonwood is most important because of the fruit's high lipid content. In fact, the pigeons depend so heavily on this food source that the availability of poisonwood fruit can determine the success of a breeding season.

White-crowned pigeons lay their two eggs in a stick nest built anywhere from ground level to high in the canopy. Both sexes share in the incubation and brooding responsibilities; males incubate during the day and females at night. Eggs hatch after two weeks of incubation. Newly hatched pigeons are fed solely with crop milk for their first few days of life, after which time fruit is added to their diet. Fruit soon becomes their primary food. Young pigeons leave the nest when they are between sixteen and twenty days old, but are fed by the parents until they are between twenty-eight to forty days old. Once they reach this age, they are capable of leaving the nesting sites and flying to feeding areas on the mainland and larger keys.

Biologists have noted that large areas of hardwood hammock (twelve acres or larger) are critical as first landing sites for young pigeons leaving their nesting areas. This observation is central to a conservation plan that proposes the protection of significant chunks of hardwood hammock habitat along the mainline keys to serve as stepping stones from the pigeons' nesting keys to the larger tropical hardwood forests on Big Pine Key and Upper Key Largo.

Little is known about the ecological requirements of white-crowned pigeons in their wintering grounds. Those birds living on Upper Key Largo seem to migrate to the Bahamas, while those living in the Lower Keys are more likely to winter in Cuba. I have seen white-crowned pigeons year-round in the Keys, but they are not nearly as plentiful as during the summer.

With no chance of getting another look at the pigeons, I clambered up the side of the solution hole and started making my way back toward the road. A swallowtail butterfly flitted down from the canopy, drifting among the tree trunks like a leaf floating amidst rocks in a slow-moving stream. It would pause briefly on a leaf tip, gently pulsing its wings before resuming flight. Its hind wings were tattered, the once-bold colors dulled with age. Schaus' swallowtail or giant swallowtail? I couldn't be certain, although chances were that it was the much more common giant.

Butterflies are integral parts of the hammock ecosystem because of their role as pollinators. Among the prettiest of the some fifty species found in Keys hammocks are the black and yellow zebra longwing, the bright orange julia butterfly, the ruddy daggerwing, and the giant swallowtail. The most famous butterfly

A Schaus' swallowtail, Adams Key, Biscayne National Park. (Photo © Thomas C. Emmel)

in the Keys, however, is the Schaus' swallowtail, a subspecies of the giant. Named in 1911 by Miami collector and physician William Schaus, the Schaus' swallowtail is internationally renowned for its beauty and rarity. This swallowtail once ranged from Miami hammocks to Lower Matecumbe Key, with some records indicating that a few butterflies may even have found their way to Key West. Destruction of hardwood hammocks and widespread spraying of insecticides for mosquito control have brought the Schaus' swallowtail to the verge of extinction. Listed as an endangered species by the state and federal governments since 1975, it is now found only in the Upper Florida Keys and on a few islands in Biscayne National Park.

Like the giant swallowtail, Schaus' swallowtail is a large, dark brown butterfly boasting bold yellow markings running in two parallel bands diagonally across the upper fore and hind wings. The upper hind wings are spotted with blue and orange on top and chestnut patches at the bottom. It can be distinguished from the giant swallowtail by its slightly smaller size and the lack of distinctive yellow spots on its tails. Eggs are laid in May and early June on torchwood and wild lime. After ten days, the eggs hatch, and the caterpillars pass through several growing stages (instars) as they feed through June and July on the tender new leaves of the host plants. After about five weeks, each caterpillar forms a hard-shelled pupa camouflaged to resemble the branch or limestone outcrop to which it is attached, becoming dormant until the following spring. Late spring rains and other subtle environmental changes stimulate each pupa to emerge, now transformed into a splendid adult butterfly. The short-lived adults are most active in the middle of the day, with males fluttering from flower to flower in search of nectar when they are not looking for females. The females do not feed, devoting their time instead to finding suitable food plants on which to lay their eggs.

Because the Schaus' swallowtail produces only one generation each year (unlike the giant swallowtail, which produces several generations), it is highly susceptible to insecticides. This, compounded by a scarcity of hardwood hammock habitat, severely limits the ability of the butterfly to increase its numbers enough to occupy more of its historic range.

The toll exacted by broad-spectrum insecticides used in mosquito control in the Keys is not limited to butterflies and other insects. Invertebrates such as the brightly colored *Liguus* tree snails (ligs) have suffered as well. Studies are being conducted to determine whether pesticide applications are responsible for the thinning of lig shells on Upper Key Largo. Many snails, especially those found near the sides of the road, have exceptionally thin shells that either crack easily or allow the animal to be seen through its shell wall. To protect the tree snails, butterflies, and other creatures in the hammocks, chemical pesticides are not used in John Pennekamp Coral Reef State Park or the Key Largo Hammock State Botanical Site.

Five major varieties of *Liguus* tree snails are found on Upper Key Largo. The snail is a listed species (species of special concern) in Florida, making it illegal to collect the shells or live snails. Ligs do not eat leaves, instead feeding on microflora (algae, fungus, and lichens) that grow on the tree trunks. They prefer seasonally deciduous trees such as Jamaica dogwood and may often be seen in masses along the upper branches of a large dogwood in the spring after their estivation. Estivation is a dry-season hibernation, when the snails find suitable branches to which they fasten themselves with mucus, sealing the entrances to their shells in the process. This mucous door protects them from drying out. If you pull a snail off its branch during estivation and break the mucous seal, it will most likely dry out and die. When warm spring rains come, rain water softens this seal, and the snails emerge from their dormant state to begin feeding.

During the wet season, a time when ligs are particularly vulnerable to predators as they move about and feed, the snails employ an interesting defense mechanism when they feel threatened. A snail that is picked up will excrete a watery, bitter-tasting liquid in the hopes of convincing whatever has picked it up to drop it. Raccoons have gotten around this defense mechanism by popping off the top three whorls of the shell and extracting the snail through the top. Birds will poke a hole in the side and pull the animal out. Other creatures that have not learned such tricks tend to leave the snails alone.

Liguus tree snails have four stalked eyes, two of which are short and two that are long. By waving the long stalked eyes around, they can distinguish movement and light. They use the small stalked eyes to feel out the path in front of them.

In the fall just before they estivate, ligs mate. They are hermaphrodites (containing both male and female organs), and after mating, both snails usually leave the encounter pregnant. Each snail comes down to the base of the tree to dig a hole in the leaf litter and lay approximately fifty pea-sized eggs. The following spring, the eggs hatch, and tiny "button" snails emerge to begin their first long trek up the tree to feed.

For its fragile tropical plants and wildlife, the hammock offers much more than sanctuary; it is home

The sounds of traffic grew louder as I neared the edge of the hammock. Through breaks in the brush, I could see cars speeding along the road, and I wondered how many of those people gazed out their car windows and ached to explore the hammock's mysterious interior as I did months before when I first passed by. I felt somehow violated by the urgency and noise of the roadside after having spent several hours wrapped in the hammock's dim green silence. For me, the hammock offers a brief interlude from the outside world, a sanctuary of sorts. For its fragile tropical plants and wildlife, the hammock offers much more than sanctuary. It is home.

The Human Touch

A lone hiker stares out at a sunset through the mangroves, National Key Deer Refuge.
(Photo © Bill Keogh)

When Key Largo's Jewfish Creek bridge is raised on a sunny weekend afternoon during the "season," traffic on both sides of U.S. 1 can back up for miles. Heatwaves shimmer across the long thin line of cars, motor homes, trailered boats, asphalt, and humanity. The scene is repeated a few miles south at the entrance to John Pennekamp Coral Reef State Park, where visitors are sometimes turned away because the park is full. Jet skis whine over shallow water flats surrounding the island, and cigarette racing boats roar across Blackwater Sound. Boats of every description filled with divers, snorkelers, fishermen, and landlubbers content to just peer over the side bob over the reefs of the Key Largo National Marine Sanctuary. Tourists crowd into tiki

Divers and snorkelers inadvertently damage coral reefs by touching the coral or standing on coral heads. Please be careful when visiting the reef! (Photo © Bill Keogh)

Urban development can spread across entire keys, leaving little forested habitat for wildlife. (Photo © Jeff Ripple)

bars, and motels proudly flash NO VACANCY in bright neon all along U.S. 1 from Key Largo to Key West. If the Keys are "Paradise," then Key Largo is the first port of call. More than four million people visit here or pass through on their way to Islamorada, Marathon, and Key West each year. Visitors to the Keys want to dive, snorkel, fish, eat, recreate, and vegetate. They may stay a day, a week, a month; some never leave. Gentle tropical breezes and bright sunshine are more than just the weather; they are a way of life.

Unfortunately, the Keys' tremendous popularity appears to be contributing to a decline in the health of many of the islands' unique ecosystems, which, regardless of their lack of neon, are still the principle attraction for most tourists. This threatens the Keys as an integrated natural community and as the foundation of the Keys' tourism-based economy. Consider the plight of the coral reefs, for instance. Coral reefs in the Keys are dying from what ecologists believe may be natural causes exacerbated by the cumulative im-

pact of sewage from the burgeoning human population, pesticides from mosquito spraying, damage from boat groundings, and intense use by divers and snorkelers. Sewage seeps from thousands of septic systems into the porous limestone bedrock, eventually finding its way out to the reef. Stormwater runoff as a rule is directly discharged into the ocean. The reefs receive a daily dose of salty, nutrient-rich water from Florida Bay, a system itself plagued by an insufficient influx of fresh water from the Everglades, unnaturally high salinity, large algal blooms, and pollution from south Florida and the Keys. Combine this with inadvertent breakage and scraping of fragile coral due to heavy visitation to most reefs by divers and snorkelers. The end result? Coral that has succumbed to blackband disease (caused by a blue-green bacteria that creates a black band of infection around the coral, killing entire colonies) or the effects of coral bleaching. Sometimes coral is replaced by thick growths of slimy, green algae rather than new coral polyps. This triggers a domino-effect that ripples through the entire coral reef community, placing local populations of reef fish and invertebrates in jeopardy. Dying reefs, fewer reef fish, and murky water are linked back to the Keys' economy because they are not conducive to memorable diving and snorkeling expeditions, a fact acknowledged by dive shop operators, charterboat captains, and others who depend on a healthy reef system to earn their living.

Seagrass beds and other nearshore communities have been affected by poor water quality and human activity as well. Pole or float a boat over the flats, and prop scars and evidence of groundings can easily be seen. When viewed from the air, the extent of prop scarring throughout the Keys is appalling. Not only is the damage an eyesore, but a whirling prop in shallow water tears seagrass from the soft bottom and churns up sediments, clouding the water. Heavy amounts of suspended sediments inhibit the ability of seagrasses to conduct photosynthesis, resulting in the death of still more plants. Leaving a scar through a seagrass bed may seem trivial to some boaters, but if you multiply each scarring by several thousand boats each year, the cumulative impact becomes quite significant. That impact is even more meaningful when you factor in the loss of some 100,000 acres of seagrass beds in Florida Bay since 1987 due to a complex combination of human-related and natural stresses.

How does the loss of seagrass beds in Florida Bay affect the ecology and economy of the Keys? Seagrass beds and mangroves support the base of the food chain for virtually every living thing in Florida Bay. Seagrass beds also provide essential cover for the juvenile phases of many commercially valuable species, including pink shrimp, blue crabs, spiny lobsters, and numerous food and game fish. The loss of seagrass habitat is bound to influence the populations of these creatures, and if current catch statistics are any indication, the future for commercial fisheries in the Keys is bleak (commercial fishing ranks second behind tourism in importance to the Keys' economic vitality). Figures from 1993 put pink shrimp harvests in the Dry Tortugas

"You call someplace Paradise, kiss it goodbye."

—the Eagles' "The Last Resort,"
from Hotel California

region at an all-time low, while sportfishing captains are decrying the abysmal fishing in many parts of Florida Bay. Somehow, the five- to seven-million-pound spiny lobster harvest (of which some 95 percent comes from the Keys) has remained steady over the last few years.

The destruction of habitat to accommodate the expanding human population in the Keys has not been limited to the reefs and seagrass beds. Mangrove forests, tropical hardwood hammocks, and pinelands have suffered from extensive deforestation to make room for hotels, shopping malls, residential areas, and the necessary infrastructure to support such development.

Deforestation itself is nothing new to the Keys; hurricanes have destroyed extensive amounts of forest over the last few thousand years. Given time, the forests can replace themselves. Even two previous periods of deforestation at the hands of humans within the last three hundred years did not leave irreparable damage. The first period occurred during the 1700s, when Bahamians harvested timber in the Upper Keys, clearing most of the valuable lumber (primarily mahogany, lignum vitae, and black ironwood) by 1769. The second period followed the Civil War, when much land was cleared for agriculture, primarily pineapple. Key limes, tomatoes, melons, sweet potatoes, and peppers were also grown.

However, we are now experiencing a third, more destructive period of deforestation. Beginning in fits and starts after the arrival of Henry Flagler's railroad in 1912, intensive development has followed deforestation, and this time the cut forests have no hope of recovery. The first subdivision was built on Key Largo in 1924, and home, retail, and urban development have continued to the present. Using aerial photography, researchers from the National Audubon Society have documented a loss of 60 percent of the mangroves in the Upper Keys between 1955 and 1985—40 percent directly from dredge-and-fill activities. Much of the remaining forest has been fragmented by a matrix of houses, roads, concrete, and exotic (non-native) ornamental vegetation. In the stretch of the Upper

Florida Keys connected by U.S. 1 from Lower Key Largo to Long Key, 41 percent of the area covered by hardwood hammock and 15 percent of the area covered by mangroves have disappeared. The isolation and fragmentation of forests alters temperature, light, wind, and water conditions within these communities to the point where they can no longer support the diversity of life they once harbored. The forests become more likely to suffer severe damage from hurricanes and are more susceptible to invasion by exotic plants. Because of the loss of vegetation, water entering estuarine and marine environments from uplands runs off more quickly and without the benefit of the slow filtering process it would have received had the forest remained intact.

The loss of forest acreage and fragmentation affect wildlife as well. The most noticeable effect is the increase in roadkills, especially among populations of reptiles and small mammals. Nesting birds are especially prone to predation by cats, as well as egg robbing by grackles and blue jays, species that thrive in an edge setting. Migratory birds that depend on forests in the Keys as stopovers for food and rest now find they have fewer places to go.

Pat Wells, the affable park manager of Lignumvitae Key State Botanical Site, is a Keys resident who has watched the decline of the Keys' environment with increasing dismay. "Several years ago, people were debating whether or not there were environmental problems in the Keys, even though long-time residents would say, 'You should have seen what it looked like here fifteen years ago.' Now people are saying, 'You should have seen what the Keys looked like five years ago.' If that's not an indication that you have a big

Garbage piled up among red mangrove roots, No Name Key. (Photo © Bill Keogh)

sun is warm and the water sparkles, the tourists will come," they say. Water sports and nightlife in a tropical setting are more than adequate to keep business bustling.

As a frequent visitor to the Keys, however, I tend to disagree. I come to swim over healthy coral reefs, fish clear waters, and wander through significant expanses of dim, green tropical hardwood forests. If I patronize the hotels, eat in the restaurants, buy bait at the tackle stores, frequent the dive shops, and otherwise support the local economy, it is because I need the services and products these businesses offer to experience the Keys' natural environment.

Fortunately, I am not alone in my point of view. Backing me up are many tourists and a large percentage of Keys residents; regional, state, and federal agencies responsible for natural resource management; and the myriad private organizations that have sprung into existence to reverse the downward spiral of the Keys' fragile ecosystems. The ecology, economy, and quality of life in the Keys are intertwined and must be managed accordingly. This means making hard deci-

environmental problem, I don't know what is."

Unfortunately, a transient society dependent on tourism for its economic survival has a problem with perspective. New residents and tourists are unfamiliar for the most part with how the Keys once looked and are oblivious to the fact that the Keys are slowly dying. To them, the water is still clear, fish still swim on the reefs, and they can find forests and wildlife if they take the time to look. The Keys still resemble the "Paradise" they expected to see. Many businesspeople refuse to acknowledge that there is a problem, thinking that bad publicity will drive visitors away. "As long as the

sions that require conservation-oriented land-use planning, correcting the mistakes of past development, and ultimately determining when the Keys can no longer support additional human development. It also means vigorously supporting strong policies for protecting the Keys from further degradation, such as those in place prohibiting offshore oil drilling near the Keys and those proposed for restoring the Everglades and Florida Bay.

Conservation programs

While it is important to gain some insight into the problems facing the Keys, it is equally important to be aware of programs and groups that have been established to preserve the Keys' natural environment. The U.S. Fish and Wildlife Service manages the Florida Keys National Wildlife Refuges, an umbrella of individual refuges that includes Crocodile Lake National Wildlife Refuge on Key Largo, the Key West and Great White Heron National Wildlife Refuges on the Gulf side of the Keys between Big Pine Key and Key West, and the National Key Deer Refuge in the Lower Keys. These refuges exist for the protection, development, and management of a network of land for wildlife habitat, with special emphasis on endangered species, migratory birds, and wetland-dependent fish. The National Park Service has established Dry Tortugas National Park (formerly Fort Jefferson National Monument) in the Dry Tortugas and Biscayne National Park in the Upper Keys north of Key Largo to protect sensitive reefs and islands. Islands in Florida Bay near the Upper Keys are protected within the boundaries of Everglades National Park.

Perhaps the most far-reaching federal conservation program in the Keys is the Florida Keys National Marine Sanctuary, which was created through the Florida Keys National Marine Sanctuary and Protection Act, enacted by Congress and signed into law by former president George Bush on November 16, 1990. This sanctuary, including Key Largo and Looe Key National Marine Sanctuaries, is managed by the National Oceanic and Atmospheric Administration (NOAA) and encompasses some 2,800 square nautical miles of th .. waters surrounding the Florida Keys and Dry Tortugas The Sanctuary prohibits oil and

gas development within its boundaries, and commercial vessel traffic is restricted within an internationally designated "Area to be Avoided." The Sanctuary is also responsible for drawing up and carrying out a management plan that, in addition to emphasizing the improvement of water quality in the area, must address these major objectives, as stated in the Sanctuary's informational literature:

- Facilitate those public and private uses of the Sanctuary that by their nature do not deplete or damage the integrity of the resources;
- Consider setting up a system of zones with varying levels of restrictions to ensure protection of resources;
- Establish regulations necessary to enforce the new plan for water quality;
- Identify the priorities for research and establish a long-term ecological monitoring program;
- Identify a variety of sources for funds needed to implement the plan and to supplement federal appropriations under the National Marine Sanctuary Program;
- Ensure coordination and cooperation between Sanctuary managers and other federal, state, and local authorities; and
- Help inform users of the Sanctuary about coral reef ecosystem conservation and navigational safety.

Multiple use is a key term for the Sanctuary, and sport and commercial fishing (with hook and line), scientific research, and recreational activities are permitted in most areas of the Sanctuary as long as they "do not undermine the fundamental health and integrity of the area."

On the state level, the Keys have nine Florida Park Service units, including John Pennekamp Coral Reef State Park and Key Largo Hammock State Botanical Site on Key Largo, Windley Key State Geologic Site in the Upper Keys, Indian Key State Historic Site and Lignumvitae Key State Botanical Site in the Matecumbe Keys, Long Key State Recreation Area at Layton, Bahia Honda State Park on Bahia Honda Key,

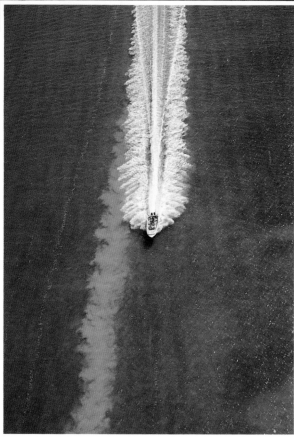

ABOVE: *The freighter* MissBeholden *being pulled off the Sambo Key reef. (Photo © Bill Keogh)* LEFT: *A boat follows the muddy path of another's propeller churning up bottom sediments in shallow water. Careless boating scars shallow-water seagrass beds, and the resulting suspended sediments can adversely affect seagrass, mangrove, and coral reef communities. (Photo © Bill Keogh)* OVERLEAF: *Yellowtop blooming on Crawl Key. This area had been cleared for development, but was purchased for conservation and will be allowed to return to its natural state. (Photo © Jeff Ripple)* OVERLEAF INSET: *Sea kayaking is a popular way to explore the backcountry of the Keys. (Photo © Jeff Ripple)*

Shell Key State Preserve in the Lower Keys, and Fort Zachary Taylor State Historic Site at Key West. The parks are managed to preserve and protect land or areas that represent "Original Natural Florida," (i.e., before the first Europeans arrived) while allowing only compatible recreation. Public access to Shell Key is prohibited, and access to Windley Key is by appointment only.

The state has also established four aquatic preserves in the Keys, which include Biscayne Bay–Card Sound Aquatic Preserve north of Key Largo; Lignumvitae Key Aquatic Preserve in the Matecumbe Keys; Coupon Bight Aquatic Preserve along the southern shoreline of Big Pine Key; and San Pedro Underwater Archaeological Preserve just south of Indian Key.

Land acquisition is critical for protecting much of the Keys from development, and several conservation groups work to help the state and federal governments acquire environmentally sensitive land for preservation. Among the organizations instrumental in acquiring land for preservation are Trust for Public Lands (TPL), Florida Keys Land and Sea Trust, and The Nature Conservancy. Both the Florida Keys Land and Sea Trust and The Nature Conservancy have purchased land and established their own sanctuaries in the Keys.

The Florida Keys Land and Sea Trust, a private, nonprofit, member-supported organization is perhaps best known for its sixty-three-acre Crane Point Hammock on Marathon. The site features the unique palm hammock with interpretive trails, a restored Conch house, and the Florida Keys Museum of Natural History. The Trust has recently expanded its programs to include marine research and environmental education.

To date, The Nature Conservancy, a national nonprofit corporation, has purchased more than six thousand acres in the Keys for preservation purposes, much of it ecologically sensitive upland areas, such as pinelands on Big Pine Key and tropical hardwood ham-

Many refuges exist for the protection, development, and management of a network of land for wildlife habitat, with special emphasis on endangered species, migratory birds, and wetland-dependent fish

mocks on North Key Largo. In the early 1970s, The Nature Conservancy provided $200,000 as a down payment on Lignumvitae Key to assist state acquisition of the island. The Nature Conservancy preserves in the Keys include the Terrestritis Preserve on Big Pine Key and Torchwood Hammock on Little Torch Key. The corporation also has developed a volunteer program for assisting agencies such as the Florida Keys Marine Sanctuary in conducting fieldwork and carrying out interpretive programs.

Some conservation organizations focus on specific areas of the Keys and support research and environmental education on these areas. One of the most successful is REEF RELIEF, a Key West-based, nonprofit group organized "to preserve and protect the living coral reef of the Florida Keys." Its programs include maintenance of more than eighty reef mooring buoys at six Key West–area reefs, public education and the operation of its environmental education center in Key West, marine debris reduction, and keeping vigil over the reef.

I realize I have touched on only a few of the topics surrounding humankind's effect on the Florida Keys. To delve into the subject in any significant detail would fill another book. My point in including this overview is to impress on everyone who spends time in the Keys that no matter how long your stay, you will make some sort of impact on the Keys' environment. You have an enormous amount of control, however, over the mark you leave. What we do to our environment today, good or bad, directly influences what will happen tomorrow and for centuries to come. "Take only pictures, leave only footprints"—you'll see plenty of signs with this message when touring parks and preserves in the Keys. Please help ensure that the tide that washes away your footprints is clean and clear, and that all living things above and below the tide line continue to have a place in "Paradise."

Black mangroves and buttonwoods, The Nature Conservancy's Torchwood Hammock Preserve. Private preserves such as this are important for conserving much of the diversity of wild lands in the Keys. (Photo © Jeff Ripple)

Appendix

Selected parks and preserves in or near the Florida Keys

National Marine Sanctuaries

Key Largo National Marine Sanctuary
MM 100 Ocean Drive, P.O. Box 1083
Key Largo, FL 33037
(305) 451-1644

Looe Key National Marine Sanctuary
216 Ann Street
Key West, FL 33040
(305) 872-4039

National Parks

Biscayne National Park
P.O. Box 1369
Homestead, FL 33090
(305) 230-7275 or (305) 230-1100

Dry Tortugas National Park
P.O. Box 6208
Key West, FL 33041
(305) 242-7700

Everglades National Park
40001 S. R. 9336
Homestead, FL 33034-6733
(305) 242-7700

National Wildlife Refuges

Crocodile Lake National Wildlife Refuge, Great White
Heron National Wildlife Refuge, Key West National Wildlife Refuge, National Key Deer Refuge (one address for
all)
P.O. Box 510
Big Pine Key, FL 33043-0510
(305) 872-2239

Florida State Park Units

Bahia Honda State Park
Route 1, Box 782
Big Pine Key, FL 33043
(305) 872-2353 or (305) 872-3897

Fort Zachary Taylor State Historic Site
P.O. Box 289
Key West, FL 33040
(305) 292-6713

Indian Key State Historic Site
P.O. Box 1052
Islamorada, FL 33036
(305) 451-8679

John Pennekamp Coral Reef State Park
P.O. Box 487
Key Largo, FL 33037
(305) 451-1202

Key Largo Hammock State Botanical Site
P.O. Box 487
Key Largo, FL 33037
(305) 451-7008

Lignumvitae Key State Botanical Site
P.O. Box 1052
Islamorada, FL 33036
(305) 451-8679

Long Key State Recreation Area
P.O. Box 776,
Long Key, FL 33001
(305) 664-4815

Florida Aquatic Preserves

Coupon Bight Aquatic Preserve; Biscayne Bay–Card Sound
Aquatic Preserve; and Lignumvitae Key Aquatic Preserve
(one address for all)
P.O. Box 2451
Key Largo, FL 33037
(305) 289-2336

San Pedro Underwater Archaeological Preserve
P.O. Box 1052
Islamorada, FL 33036
(305) 451-8679

Florida Keys Land and Sea Trust

Crane Point Hammock Museum, Florida Keys Children's
Museum, and Museum of Natural History of the Florida
Keys (one address for all)
P.O. Box 536
5550 Overseas Highway
Marathon, FL 33050
(305) 743-9100 or (305) 743-3900

References

A *Video Guide to the Fish and Marine Life of the Caribbean, Bahamas, and Florida.* Miami: Video Fish Book, 1990. VHS, 45 minutes.

Alevizon, William, and Dennis Landmeier. "Variability in the population structures of four western Atlantic parrotfishes." *Environmental Biology of Fishes* 10(3):149–158, 1984.

Audubon, Maria R. *Audubon and His Journals, Vol. II.* Freeport, New York: Books for Libraries Press, reprinted 1972.

Bancroft, G. Thomas. "A Closer Look: White-crowned Pigeon." *Birding* 24(1):21–24, 1992.

Carson, Rachel. *The Edge of the Sea.* Boston: Houghton Mifflin Company, 1955.

Gato, Jeannette, ed. *The Monroe County Environmental Story.* Big Pine Key: The Monroe County Environmental Education Task Force, 1991.

Goreau, Thomas F., Nora I. Goreau, and Thomas J. Goreau. "Corals and Coral Reefs." *Scientific American* 241(2):124–136, 1979.

Haynes, Bill. Personal interview with author. November 1993.

Herrnkind and Mark J. Butler IV. "Factors regulating postlarval settlement and juvenile microhabitat use by spiny lobsters *Panulirus argus*." *Marine Ecology Progress Series* 34:23–30, November 1986.

Hoffmeister, John Edward. *Land from the Sea: Geologic Story of South Florida.* Coral Gables: University of Miami Press, 1974.

Hutchings, P.A. "Biological Destruction of Coral Reefs." *Coral Reefs* 4:239–252, 1986.

Izaak Walton League of America (Florida Keys Chapter). *Wetlands of the Florida Keys.* Pamphlet.

Kaplan, Eugene H. *Coral Reefs.* Peterson Field Guides. Boston: Houghton Mifflin, 1982.

Kaplan, Eugene H. *Southeastern and Caribbean Seashores.* Peterson Field Guides. Boston: Houghton Mifflin, 1988.

Levi, Herbert W. "Orb-Weaving Spiders and Their Webs." *American Scientist* 66:739–742, November-December, 1978.

Multer, H. Gray. *Seakeys Habitat Guide to the Florida Keys National Marine Sanctuary: Past, Present, Future.* Florida Institute of Oceanography, 1993.

Myers, Ronald L., and John J. Ewel, eds. *Ecosystems of Florida.* Orlando: University Presses of Florida, 1990.

Newbert, Christopher. *Within a Rainbowed Sea.* Hillsboro, Oregon: Beyond Words Publishing, Inc., 1990.

Parks, Jeanne. Personal interview with author. January 1993.

Parks, Jeanne. Personal interview with author. 26 April, 1993.

Ross, Michael S., *et al.* "Sea Level Rise and the Reduction in Pine Forests in the Florida Keys." (Unpublished document.)

Strong, Allan M., and G. Thomas Bancroft. "Patterns of Deforestation and Fragmentation of Mangrove and Deciduous Seasonal Forests in the Upper Florida Keys." (Unpublished document.)

Strong, Allan M., and G. Thomas Bancroft. "Postfledging Dispersal of White-crowned Pigeons (*Columba leucocephala*): Implications for Conservation of Deciduous Seasonal Forests in the Florida Keys." (Unpublished document.)

Thomas, Lowell P. "What's Happening to Florida's Reefs?" *Rodale's Scuba Diving* 52–56, August 1993.

Tuskes, Dr. Paul M. "Population Structure and Biology of *Liguus* Tree Snails on Lignumvitae Key, Florida." *The Nautilus* 95(4):162–169, 1981.

Voss, Gilbert L. *Coral Reefs of Florida.* Sarasota, Florida: Pineapple Press, 1988.

Wells, Pat. Personal interview with author. April 1993.

Index

A giant tree cactus growing in a hardwood hammock. This endangered, shade-loving cactus may reach heights of fifteen to twenty feet. (Photo © Jeff Ripple)

Author Notes

(Photo © Renée Ripple)

(Photo © Tim Reese)

Jeff Ripple, a natural history writer and photographer, has devoted the last several years to exploring and photographing natural areas of Florida, including Big Cypress Swamp, the Ten Thousand Islands, the Everglades, and the Florida Keys.

Jeff's photography outside of Florida has been primarily in the Great Smoky Mountains. His work has been used by the National Park Service, U.S. Department of Fish and Wildlife, Florida Division of Parks and Recreation, National Audubon Society, The Nature Conservancy, Defenders of Wildlife, and other conservation organizations. Publication credits include *Backpacker, Birder's World, Nature Photographer, Defenders, Florida Wildlife,* and *Boca Raton Magazine. The Florida Keys—The Natural Wonders of an Island Paradise* is Jeff's second book. His first, *Big Cypress Swamp and the Ten Thousand Islands,* was published by the University of South Carolina Press.

Jeff, his wife Renée, and their cats Tabatha, Suwannee, and Bailey live near Gainesville, Florida.

Bill Keogh, adventure travel photographer, has had his home base on Big Pine Key of the Florida Keys for the past decade. His travels over the continental United States, the Carribean, and Central America have only reinforced his feelings about the Florida Keys' uniqueness. As a contract photographer for Newfound Harbor Marine Institute at Seacamp, a marine science educational facility, he works with groups who are excited about the Florida Keys environment.

Bill's photos have been utilized by many keys environmental groups including The Nature Conservancy, who in 1993 awarded him a conservation colleague award for photographic contributions. Others who have used his work include the National Park Service, U.S. Fish and Wildlife Service, National Geographic Society, National Marine Sanctuary, and World Wildlife Fund. His publication credits include *Scuba Diving, Wooden Boat, Yacht, Backpacker, Seakayaker, Islands,* and *Wilderness.*

Bill's favorite place in the keys is two hundred feet above them, with his Nikon, a brick of Fujichrome, and the back door open on the Piper Tripacer.

OVERLEAF: *Red mangroves at sunset, Big Pine Key, National Key Deer Refuge. (Photo © Bill Keogh)*